WABI-SABI WELCOME

WABI-SABI WELCOME

Learning to embrace the imperfect
and entertain with thoughtfulness and ease

JULIE POINTER ADAMS

ARTISAN | NEW YORK

Library of Congress Cataloging-in-Publication Data

Names: Adams, Julie Pointer, author.
Title: Wabi-sabi welcome / Julie Pointer Adams.
Description: New York : Artisan, 2017.
Identifiers: LCCN 2016038085 | ISBN 9781579656997
(hardback, paper over board)
Subjects: LCSH: Interior decoration—Psychological aspects.
| Entertaining.
Classification: LCC NK2113.A33 2017 | DDC 747.001/9—dc23
LC record available at https://lccn.loc.gov/2016038085

Cover design by Michelle Ishay-Cohen
Design by Charlotte Heal

Artisan books are available at special discounts when
purchased in bulk for premiums and sales promotions as
well as for fund-raising or educational use. Special editions
or book excerpts also can be created to specification. For
details, contact the Special Sales Director at the address
below, or send an e-mail to specialmarkets@workman.com.

For speaking engagements, contact speakersbureau
@workman.com.

Published by Artisan
A division of Workman Publishing Co., Inc.
225 Varick Street
New York, NY 10014-4381
artisanbooks.com

Artisan is a registered trademark of
Workman Publishing Co., Inc.

Published simultaneously in Canada by
Thomas Allen & Son, Limited

Printed in China

10 9 8 7 6 5 4

To Mom and Dad—for consistently modeling what
sincere humility, hospitality, and an open, generous life truly look like.

.

And to Ryan—for being a constant source of joy and encouragement, and for
happily building a welcoming home full of wabi-sabi pleasures by my side.

CONTENTS

Introduction   11

A Closer Look at Wabi-Sabi   18

Where to Begin   24

Chapter One | Japan   31

Chapter Two | Denmark   73

Chapter Three | California   111

Chapter Four | France   169

Chapter Five | Italy   213

Epilogue   260

Resources   262

Acknowledgments   266

Index   270

INTRODUCTION

Entertaining, in the traditional sense, can feel overwhelming—even intimidating—with so many things to consider: whom to invite, what to cook, what dishware to use, how to style the table, and more. But what if being a good host meant little more than sharing a cup of tea on the porch, or merely creating a warm, welcoming environment for your guests? Entertaining is first and foremost about being together, no matter how, when, or where, rather than trying to impress our guests or achieve perfection. Creating this more generous and more forgiving definition of entertaining is what *Wabi-Sabi Welcome* is all about.

I wrote this book for anyone hungry to share his or her home and life in a simpler, less perfection-seeking way. Regrettably, I've found that the easier it is to connect through devices, the less and less aware we are of the importance of being connected to the people right around us, and the more intimidated we are by how polished everyone else's lives look. We've forgotten how good it is to have unhurried, uncurated experiences in the company of others, in real time, with real conversation. These pages are a reminder that all entertaining requires is a bit of

thoughtfulness in order to make our homes the kind of intimate and comfy spaces that people love to gather in, and how rich our lives become when we take the time to regularly open our doors.

The Japanese aesthetic of wabi-sabi leads us to such a version of entertaining. This book explores what wabi-sabi looks and feels like, showing how and where I've experienced it across the globe. So what is it, and why does it matter? It's a way of life that celebrates the *perfectly imperfect*—beauty found in unusual, unfashionable places or objects, and in moments usually overlooked or unappreciated. It can be found in lovely places, too, perhaps just not where we most expect it. Most important, this mind-set is about paying attention. It is the habit of noticing and relishing small and hidden wonders, like a peony dropping its petals or a church bell tolling at dinnertime. It's a willingness to be easily delighted instead of critical, skeptical, or fearful. Wabi-sabi is candid, honest, and unswerving from the everydayness of real life, and it can liberate us from the burden of expectation because it always welcomes the unexpected. Embracing wabi-sabi as we entertain gives us license to reorder our priorities,

letting go of what we think is required of us and replacing it with our own version of what special and meaningful look like on our own terms.

We need wabi-sabi in our homes and minds now more than ever because we are over-saturated with glossy images of "perfection"—there's far too much in the media to compare ourselves to, seemingly always telling us to do more. A wabi-sabi viewpoint pushes these ideals aside and urges us to appreciate a different kind of ideal, such as people, places, and things with humility and simplicity, giving little importance to what's perceived as cool or of-the-moment. People who embrace wabi-sabi live large, open lives, with welcoming homes in which to enter-tain at a moment's notice. Entertaining comes easily to them because their idea of hosting is about simply showing up, not showing off. You know these individuals by the way they make you feel instantly at ease and at home. Whether they offer you grilled squid or a glass of apple juice, the crux of the matter for them is provid-ing real comfort and deep connection rather than adhering to conventional ideas of what entertaining should be.

My personal sense of what sharing a home is all about changed dramatically after my family's house burned down in a California wildfire, and with it nearly everything we owned. Whereas at times I may have been tempted to buy into the idea that what I owned, and how perfectly I controlled it all, defined me, I swiftly learned on the brink of adulthood how temporary stuff is. Instead of desiring the best, most covetable, or most sophisticated objects, I've come to see my home as a vessel for filling with friends and belongings that remind me of transience, such as traces of nature, photographs, and gifts from loved ones. I still enjoy and admire things, and my current home is full of them, but they're more like props than praiseworthy possessions—aids for making my home as warm and welcoming as possible. Objects are fleeting, but so is the time we have with others, and home is the place for making the most of our valuable moments together.

While wabi-sabi is an expansive, inclusive way of seeing the world, it's far from willy-nilly. It's a thoughtful, intentional aesthetic (even if the intent is to let things age naturally) that takes shape in many different forms, which is why I was inspired to create this collection of wabi-sabi expressions from around the world. Each chapter is framed by a wabi-sabi principle and explores different regions where these principles are practiced: Japan, Denmark, California, France, and Italy. You'll see the young and the old, families and single people who have woven wabi-sabi into their everyday being, expressing this philosophy whether at home alone or entertaining a small crowd. These pages are filled with the real and raw things of life—friends, homes, and settings captured just as I found them, shot exclusively on film to reveal flaws and imperfections. No editing, enhancing, or embellishing here. Instead, you'll find down-to-earth ideas for making anyone feel more at home in your space, and simple, approachable recipes that I know to be reliable fallbacks for meals that can feed two or ten. Ultimately, this book should be used like a field guide, both for browsing and reading. I hope it lives somewhere in your home where dog-earing and underlining happen naturally, getting smudged up as you cook and acquiring a perfectly wabi-sabi patina.

Bringing people together shouldn't feel complicated or contrived; it should be joyful and spontaneous. This book is meant to inspire you to make those joyful, spontaneous moments of togetherness happen more often. Having a community is an essential and basic part of life, and for the most part we all have the same joys, desires, and fears—we want to be known, to belong somewhere, and to share the big and little things in life with others. Sometimes we simply need to be with people to feel seen and heard again, and making our homes a healing place for that to happen is a beautiful way to begin. I hope this book can serve as a reminder that so much contentment and conviviality can be added to our lives when we open our homes and ourselves—perfectly imperfect as we are—to friends, family, neighbors, and strangers. The wabi-sabi way will help get us there.

A CLOSER LOOK AT **WABI-SABI**

The concept of wabi-sabi is deeply rooted in Japan, though you won't find the term in the dictionary there, and even many Japanese people find it very difficult to describe.

The idea developed when two separate words, *wabi* and *sabi*, were joined to convey a certain look, feeling, and world perspective. *Wabi* means something like simplicity, humility, and living in tune with nature; it describes someone who is content with little and makes the most of whatever he or she has, always moving toward having less. *Sabi*, on the other hand, refers to what happens with the passage of time; it's about transience and the beauty and authenticity of age. Practicing *sabi* is learning to accept the natural cycle of growth and death, as well as embracing the imperfections that come with this progression. Together, *wabi* and *sabi* form a feeling that finds harmony and serenity in what is uncomplicated, unassuming, mysterious, and fleeting.

Wabi-sabi has often been tied to the Japanese tea ceremony, a ritual that demonstrates the mindfulness and modesty needed to fully understand this way of living. But wabi-sabi isn't just for Zen monks and tea masters—anyone can exercise this mind-set. It's about recognizing beauty in the perfectly imperfect, and understanding that authentic loveliness can be found in many surprising places.

It's hard to get a feel for wabi-sabi if you've never encountered it before, but it should be noted that this aesthetic isn't junky, messy, or shoddy. It's also not shabby chic—you won't find new items intentionally distressed in order to look antique. Instead, the beauty of wabi-sabi appears when age and time are allowed to take their intended course; you might see it in a weathered barn, a withering tree, or a wrinkly face. It's the magic of something completely temporary and transcendent: a frog leaping into the water, moonlight on crashing waves, old friends gathered for a brief reunion. It's not just a visual style, either; we can experience wabi-sabi when we incorporate its principles (which will be explored in the following chapters) into our everyday lives, which is why I believe it's such a natural part of practicing genuine hospitality. Although identifying wabi-sabi isn't always a black-and-white endeavor, the following examples may help you recognize in your own home and habits what is and isn't wabi-sabi.

A CLOSER LOOK AT WABI-SABI

WABI-SABI

NOT WABI-SABI

Dried flowers or branches

Cracked or chipped pottery

Solid wooden rocking chairs

Softly glowing/diffused light from
a lantern, candles, or a fire

Things that inspire contentment or
longing (like natural beauty
or something melancholy)

Aged, faded, and scuffed wood

Flea-market items

Rust or signs of decay

Wrinkled linen napkins

Rough and uneven stone walls

Quilts with patches and frayed hems

Soft overstuffed chairs with lumpy
feather pillows

One-of-a-kind art pieces (whether a
child's drawing or an original sculpture)

Worn leather bags or shoes with a patina

A wardrobe with a few timeless, long-lasting
items you wear again and again

Belongings that reflect personality and
meaning (like photos, books, letters,
and collected treasures)

Irregular, nonuniform surfaces (like a
stone wall, a forest floor covered in
leaves, or a mossy tiled roof)

Dappled light

Cozy, intimate spaces

Layers of faded, nuanced paint

Fake flowers or plants

Stained or cracking plastic

Sleek, high-tech office chairs

Weak light from fluorescents
or fake candles

Things that spark envy in us (like a
flashy car or a showy house)

Peeling and cracked laminate or linoleum

Giant warehouse discount stores

New, perfectly polished materials

Solid steel fences

Synthetic bedding

Rigid wingback chairs upholstered
with silk and tassels

Mass-marketed reproductions

Cracking imitation leather

An overstuffed closet full of items
you wear only once or twice a year

Belongings purchased as status symbols

Slick, shiny, homogenous surfaces

Strong, harsh, bright light

Large, empty, echoey rooms

Bold, bright, glossy lacquer

A CLOSER LOOK AT WABI-SABI

WHERE TO BEGIN

Just as hospitality is universal, the wabi-sabi way can be adopted anywhere, transforming how we see beauty, make our homes, and entertain.

Although this book explores very specific places where I've experienced facets of wabi-sabi, there are countless other cultures that could be exemplary models—they simply haven't been a part of my own personal journey thus far. And because wabi-sabi can be embodied by anyone, no matter the time or place, this concept also represents many ideas that cannot be confined or attributed to just one region of the globe. The following are some basic principles that are found in the places included in the book, but they also extend beyond and can be carried with you anywhere you practice being a warm, hospitable host.

Wabi-Sabi Starts at Home
—

Home is a natural training ground for practicing a more wabi-sabi way of life, because our homes are usually where we feel safest and most at ease being entirely ourselves. In my own process of moving away from *perfect* and toward *perfectly imperfect*, I've discovered that the ideas explored in this book help make my daily life feel simpler,

more thoughtful, and more carefree. This is because at its core, wabi-sabi teaches us to cling to what's essential, and to forget the rest. It also helps us to reexamine what "essential" really means, and there's no better place to do this than in our private spaces. Focusing on what's most important can aid us in everything we do at home: taking care of our families, decorating, entertaining, cooking meals, relaxing, and so on. Our dwellings are mirrors of ourselves, and the way we create and share them always reflects what we believe in and care about—from day-to-day trivialities to big, significant decisions. For me, the more personal, meaningful, and perfectly imperfect I allow my home to be, the less consumed I am with trying to "keep up" with trendy designs or anyone else's version of what home should be. Likewise, when I concentrate on hosting humbly rather than trying to impress, my ego fades and I can pour my energy into making my guests feel as welcome as possible. Hopefully you will find, as I have, that bringing this way of being into your home inspires a deep sigh of relief.

Make Time to Be Together
—

Choosing what's essential, as wabi-sabi encourages us to do, requires taking a hard look at our priorities and making some sacrifices along the way. No matter how often I've tried, I always come back to the conclusion that I simply can't have it all, and in order to make way for what I really want—which is rich relationships and warm hospitality in my home—I have to let some other things go. Like many people, however, I'm not immune to chronic busyness, when life is full but not always extraordinarily deep. Living a mindful, considered life means making time and space to breathe, slow down, and be specific about what I truly desire. For most of us, this involves quality time shared with others. So instead of filling your calendar with countless weekend coffee dates, you might reserve Sundays as a time to eat, read, and enjoy leisure time with people who are really important to you. It could also mean that when you *do* get time with friends, you concentrate on really being together rather than diddle away the moments on social media or small talk. For others, it might simply mean committing one night a week to having someone over, in spite of how busy work or family life happens to be. I've found that regardless of my circumstances, my most fulfilling times are when my relationships are flourishing, but this always requires saying no to something else or, in some cases, many things.

Keeping to this habit of spending quality time with others might involve telling someone else of your intention so they can hold you accountable, or simply writing it down for yourself as a tangible reminder; some years ago I was gifted a small "wish book" in which I wrote many desires, and since then, all of them have come to fruition, including having more time to spend with loved ones. Sometimes it just takes reminding yourself of what you really want and what's most important in order to make it happen. I'm always happy to discover that despite how pressing other matters may seem, investing in togetherness richly rewards me every time.

Make Do with What You Have

—

Wabi-sabi is about humbly making do with whatever you have and, in doing so, experiencing beauty in unexpected places. Maybe you live in a tiny studio apartment that will never resemble the homes featured in magazines, blogs, and books. Or perhaps you live in a larger home and aren't sure how to incorporate this uncluttered way of living. None of this matters: wabi-sabi can be for you, too. It's a mind-set that helps you move toward needing fewer objects and material possessions to make you happy.

However, wabi-sabi isn't about getting rid of everything you own—we live in a material world, after all. Instead, it's about recognizing the pleasure we can experience from what we *do* have, without constantly needing to acquire more. And though the concept may be tied to a particular aesthetic, I think the really important components of wabi-sabi—like humility, contentment, and awareness—can transform anyone. Wabi-sabi inspires us to be resourceful and creative with whatever we've been given and to express gratitude by joyfully sharing it with others.

Focus Fully on Your Guests

—

Wabi-sabi is largely about learning to pay better attention; it's a daily practice of mindfulness, meditation, and seeing everything around us more clearly. I'll be the first to admit that my attention span isn't what it used to be and that I'm constantly fighting against the temptation to be entertained at every moment. I find myself skimming paragraphs, scrolling distractedly through my phone, and generally processing about ten things at a time. Though it's easy to blame technology, too many responsibilities, and a constant string of interruptions, the real problem is me! I've realized that potential diversions will always be there, so it's up to me to figure out how to focus on what's important. When it comes to being with another person, this means putting away or turning off anything— cell phones, cameras, tablets, the television, talk radio—that's going to create an obstacle to truly engaging. And while being fully attentive to guests isn't exactly a novel idea, I think we need this reminder now more than ever, at a time when we're able to sit in a room with one person, while also being connected with tens, hundreds, thousands, or even millions of other people all at once. The wabi-sabi way can be a helpful antidote to this scatterbrained approach to living, reminding us of the extraordinary value of taking in just one simple thing at a time.

Let Guests Participate

—

Welcoming guests into your home is a beautiful opportunity to create a sense of belonging, and one of the best ways to inspire this feeling is to let them participate. This can be a fine line to walk, since company should feel totally taken care of, but I think inviting people to play a part in your home or special occasion (besides just showing up, of course) means that they leave with a distinct sense of having contributed. Whether that means bringing a bottle of wine, arranging a bouquet, tossing the salad, or watching the kids in the backyard, participating makes everyone more present and attentive and allows your guests to get involved rather than passively consume the experience. And while you may have friends who would rather just kick back, I generally find that people feel more comfortable when they have a specific role to fulfill. Embracing wabi-sabi also frees us from feeling as though everything must be picture-perfect when guests arrive; though it's perhaps an unconventional approach to entertaining etiquette, I think giving your friends or family the sense of being needed is more important than placing dinner on the table the moment they arrive (though you probably shouldn't leave the entire meal for visitors to prepare). A good way to get everyone involved is to take a moment to think about what unique talent each guest might be able to contribute— who knows a killer salad dressing recipe? who has exceptional taste in cheese?—and make use of that talent. You'll find that asking visitors to contribute their gifts is truly a gift to them!

Japan

Chapter One

QUIETLY, HUMBLY, **MODESTLY**

Be Down-to-Earth and Welcoming, Warmhearted and Never Pretentious

In Japan, entertaining reflects a truly modest approach to life. Hosts bow to guests, and meals begin with a phrase that means "I humbly receive." The culture teaches that hosting with humility creates a welcoming, comfortable place for visitors; simple gatherings become meaningful through ritual and mindfulness, and people are fully attentive to one another. The ancient Japanese tradition of the tea ceremony expresses these values perfectly through the careful, considered way the tea master serves guests with only the most necessary elements in a small, sparse room. This quiet practice shows that hosting can be straightforward, uncluttered, and wonderfully unassuming.

When we prune hospitality to its essentials, as the Japanese do so elegantly, we realize that a listening ear and undistracted care are often all that's needed. Wabi-sabi encourages us to act naturally, sincerely, and with ease so that we can focus on what's important to our guests, and let go of controlling the situation or obsessing over details. In the hope of bringing this more humble, gracious hospitality into my home, I have taped to my wall a reminder from writer Simone Weil that "attention is the rarest and purest form of generosity."

It should come as no surprise that the wabi-sabi concept derives from Japan, since it's all about making modest, examined choices in every part of life: in our homes, with our resources, even in what we consider to be beautiful. My impression of Japanese culture is that it teaches people to not only be satisfied with little but to also be grateful. Such an approach is the key to living humbly, allowing us to be generous with whatever we have—whether that's time or money or merely a sunny outlook on life—because we recognize that everything we have is a gift. The everyday habits explored in this chapter are just some of the ways I've witnessed how to make warm, openhanded entertaining a genuine way of life. You may find, as I have, that emulating this gentle, giving attitude leaves you with the feeling of having infinitely more, not less.

*Nobu and Erina abandoned a busy urban life to move
to the quiet, mountainous countryside near a town called
Sasayama with their son, Haruto, and daughter, Kiko.
They regularly and generously welcome friends and
guests from the city, and run a beautiful shop called
Archipelago.*

The Humble Host
Begin by Bowing
—

Bowing is extremely important in Japan, where it's seen as a way of showing respect and deference toward others. Japanese culture is full of practical acts that encourage modesty, like crouching through miniature doorways to enter a tearoom, sitting on child-sized stools to shower and bathe, or regularly giving gifts as a way of expressing gratitude. These actions help keep us down-to-earth by showing us how close we are (literally!) to the ground, and reminding us to be thoughtful of others. But the purpose of bowing to friends and new acquaintances isn't just physical; like wabi-sabi, it's about embracing a new mind-set and attitude that can change the way we entertain. Being grounded helps us focus on what's most important without getting distracted along the way.

While most of us are not in the habit of literally bowing (and I'm not necessarily suggesting that you start now), we have other forms of etiquette that influence how we treat one another. I've encountered several Japanese hosts who demonstrated bowing by going well out of their way to drive me long distances, cook nourishing meals, and show me around their towns and cities. Maybe for you, "bowing" is being extra sensitive to a friend's allergies, willingly accommodating them even when it seems like a hassle. Or it's squeezing in an uninvited last-minute guest and not making a big deal about it. If you're known for being a talker, bowing might mean taking the backseat in a conversation and listening without interruption. I've had to learn (and relearn, many times) how valuable it is to set aside my own expectations in order to accommodate the needs of my guests, whether that means giving them more (or less) food, conversation, time, energy, empathy, or space. Entertaining is ultimately about making our guests happy, and when we focus on doing that, we'll find our own joy along the way.

Prepare Ahead Like a Tea Master

—

Much like being a Japanese tea master, hosting can be an intricate art form with lots of different parts to consider. Even though the act of serving tea may appear simple, a formal tea host takes it upon himself to practice extensively and to become familiar with poetry, the arts, crafts, gardening, arranging flowers, and cooking, while also learning to become more graceful, more selfless, and more attentive to the needs of others. The purpose of all this preparation is for the master to be able to fully engage with his guests in a variety of ways. Likewise, even the casual entertainer should plan ahead so that when friends arrive, he or she can completely relax, enjoy togetherness, and thoughtfully meet whatever needs arise.

Advance preparation might mean borrowing extra chairs from a neighbor, lighting candles or incense, gathering fresh foliage from the yard, making a playlist, or tidying up. Or for extra-special occasions, it could mean enlisting your guests to participate somehow beforehand.

Recently, a friend told me about a dinner she held for a handful of close friends who were asked to bring a found or homemade item for a gift exchange; her teenage son went a step further and typed up three uplifting adjectives about each person to be placed on his or her plate. A simple, caring gesture like this can be much more memorable and meaningful than an elaborate tablescape (though there's a time and place for that, too). Alternatively, if you're an overplanner, preparing ahead could mean sitting with a glass of wine before your guests arrive, simply so you won't be tempted to clean the mirrors one more time. Wherever you fall on the spectrum, planning means that you aren't preoccupied with last-minute preparations when people arrive. Instead, be single-minded in addressing the task at hand, which is above all to be warm and attentive.

Slow Down and Quiet Your Mind

—

A wabi-sabi perspective requires a slower, quieter approach to life than we may be used to, similar to the sensation that Japanese Zen gardens are meant to inspire. Zen gardens are small, hushed, subtle spaces with few visual distractions—unlike people in much of the modern world, the Japanese are not afraid of deep silence. The purpose of these gardens is to encourage meditation, and the way we approach them can be a metaphor for how we look at everything else. If we're still, focused, and content, we see an abundance of beauty. But if we're impatient, rushed, or bored in this tranquil space, we'll miss the whole point.

The same might be said for entertaining. Slowing down is a way to make time and space to enjoy rare moments of peace and togetherness, and it's difficult to be thoughtful while moving at a frenetic pace. When I hurry through meals, rush through conversations, check my phone again and again, or squander moments of rest and relaxation, the whole day feels like one diversion after another. Being constantly preoccupied makes my mind so noisy that I no longer hear or see what's going on around me.

Slowing down means readjusting our expectations of what we can fit into a day. Hospitality doesn't abide by a schedule, and while we may feel compelled to plan each hour, doing this makes us miss opportunities to really connect with those around us. So how do we break the habit? Start making just one or two commitments on Saturdays instead of five or six. Let Sunday be a day of rest, or a "free-range" day to go wherever you want with whomever you want, without the confines of an agenda or a long to-do list. Sit on the porch reading with a friend for hours, or let a lazy brunch extend into the afternoon. Invite friends or family over on a whim for dinner or a piece of pie. My favorite way to slow down usually involves abandoning my to-do lists and instead spending a long, laid-back Saturday at the beach (or the park, river, or lake) with a handful of friends, and then heading home with the crew for a mellow cookout or a potluck. Balancing our chaotic calendars with quiet reprieves is ultimately what will help us simplify our homes, minds, and lives.

The Humble Home
Celebrate Humble Materials
—

Material choices are involved on almost every level in our homes, and wabi-sabi inspires us to be selective with every decision. It favors having fewer but longer-lasting and higher-quality possessions; items that get better with age and can be somewhat easily repaired. Such things are often made from what I consider to be humble materials because they're raw and natural, requiring little processing before they're put to use. Think wood, wool, clay, rough paper, bamboo, flax or linen, leather, stone, woven grass, and iron—all subject to wear, nicks, tears, cracks, and rust. Compare them to items that are shiny, glossy, and uniform, like plastic, glass, polyester, particleboard, and other synthetic materials, and you'll start to see the difference.

Choosing materials based on what's most unrefined and enduring changes how we buy things—it may affect how you select dishes and furnishings, clothes, decor, appliances, storage containers, cleaning supplies, even toys and recreational items. Unfortunately, items made from "humble" materials are, ironically, often the most expensive, because man-made materials are commonly so much cheaper to produce. And because most mass-produced objects are designed to fall apart or stop working after a fairly short time, we have to buy them again and again. Over time, they end up costing us more than if we'd bought a better-quality item in the first place!

Investing in humble materials may mean giving up the ability to shop whenever we want. However, whether we like acquiring new sets of sheets or summer dresses, celebrating things that are made with integrity inspires us to look at the long term; it's the big picture versus the *right now*. What table linens will I want to have for years to come, even when they're faded and need repairs? What silverware will I be happy to pass on to someone? Will a wooden mixing spoon serve me longer than a cheaper plastic version? How will a woven sea-grass rug reflect wear and tear versus one made of synthetic fibers? Based on my budget, I've always opted to scour places like thrift stores and estate sales, and to save up for what I can't find secondhand. My approach has been that if I can afford only a cheap version of something I really want (both cost- and quality-wise), I go without it until I can save enough to buy the higher-quality piece. And by quality I don't mean designer clothes or furniture that's marked up simply because it carries a brand name, but rather things made from good materials that I know will get better over time.

This tactic makes nearly everything I own seem very special. Though my cupboard, closet, and living room may be sparer than some, I find that having fewer but well-loved things teaches me to be more content with what I have—and helps me more readily share them with whoever comes to my home.

OPPOSITE

These relaxed arrangements are good reference points for wabi-sabi-inspired flowers—borrowing elements from both conventional floral arranging and traditional Japanese ikebana. They were created by Tokyo-based florist Chieko Ueno, who owns a floral shop and business called Forager.

Let Flowers Fade and Fall

—

Practicing wabi-sabi means learning to see that uniquely unusual is more valuable than traditionally pretty, and that impermanence is part of what makes things intriguing and appealing. Wabi-sabi embraces dying as a necessary part of life. Such acceptance allows age to enhance beauty rather than diminish it, because beauty comes from time, wisdom, and experience. While this outlook applies to everything from objects to people, one very practical way to introduce it into your life is to change the way you think about flowers.

A good place to start is the Japanese art form of *ikebana*. Though this version of flower arranging is multilayered, it's essentially about creating minimal, balanced compositions that help us appreciate simple elegance. Unlike traditional Western bouquets, an ikebana arrangement might include only one flowering branch, petal-less flowers, withered leaves, or open seedpods—things, namely, that we might feel compelled to reject or toss, but that a wabi-sabi mind-set considers most interesting. When we allow living things to fade in full view, we welcome loveliness in transience. Wilting but still-fragrant jasmine or a single, brittle olive branch will always be more special than artificial silk roses that last forever. Likewise, stringing a fading eucalyptus garland from the porch rafters, or hanging a wreath woven from wild vines on the front door, imparts more character than any pristine but fake version could ever achieve. And keeping dried hydrangeas or curled birch bark and cattail fluff around the house doesn't suggest that you're sloppy or negligent—it shows an appreciation for every stage of life. Living things are always changing, and those changes can be truly extraordinary.

ABOVE

*The corners of Nobu's home office are filled
with beautiful handmade treasures collected
from various places and people.*

OPPOSITE

*Chef Yuri Nomura's home is decorated with a
mix of timeworn, timeless pieces, along with
modern furniture, artwork, and appliances,
creating a seamless blend of old and new.*

Have House Slippers for Guests

—

Removing shoes is usually associated with entering a sacred space or seeking relief, and our homes should provide both of these sensations. In Japan, removing one's shoes before entering a home is a deeply ingrained cultural norm; in the past, almost all activities in the Japanese home (eating, sitting, sleeping) centered on the floor made of delicate woven mats, so it was very important to have clean feet at all times. While some of those traditions have since become more Westernized and moved off the floor, leaving shoes at the door still represents relaxation, respect, and an effort to keep dirt and dust outside.

It's a testament to Japanese hospitality that after asking them to remove their shoes, hosts often provide slippers for their guests. This custom of supplying "outsiders" with slippers instantly makes everyone feel more welcome. On the few occasions I've been lucky enough to experience it, it's always made me feel like an honored guest or a part of the family. Silly as it may seem, wearing the same footwear as everyone else can provide that feeling of belonging we often crave. On cold mornings or around the winter holidays, my entire family can be found in either sheepskin boots or puffy, feather-filled slippers we call "foot duvets." We may not look particularly chic or sophisticated, but that's hardly the point. What matters is that looking goofy together keeps us humble and helps us feel cozy and comfortable whether we're at our home or someone else's.

While some folks like to keep their shoes on, once they notice that everyone else is shoeless or slippered, they usually follow suit. Having suitable footwear on hand for visitors doesn't have to be expensive. You can often find affordable versions of cotton, woven-grass, or leather slippers in Asian markets, big import shops, or, of course, online. This small gesture can be a no-brainer way of making sure that anyone who steps through your door feels instantly at home.

The Humble Table

Seek Out the Handmade

—

Handmade items reveal the human touch; even when created with the utmost precision, they always have some irregularities or what we might think of as flaws. But these touches of character are precisely what sets wabi-sabi objects apart. Think of a heavy walnut cutting board with obvious knots, a wooden spoon with a wonky handle, a clay jar with dips and grooves in the surface, a hand-stitched garment, or a quilt with painstakingly delicate hems. That cutting board might have been an experiment by your father, and the clay pot might be your first attempt at the wheel in ceramics class. They may look somewhat amateurish, but that naive, irregular quality is exactly what makes us prize these singular objects.

Wabi-sabi objects are valuable only when they're doing what they're made to do, so rare china that's too priceless to be used doesn't count as wabi-sabi. In general, functional, organically shaped, textured, simply designed (or *un-designed*) pieces found in matte and muted shades do. Having said all that, there's no hard-and-fast rule for what qualifies as wabi-sabi. Vague as it is, the best indicator that an object has a wabi-sabi spirit is that it doesn't draw attention to itself. While a violet velour tablecloth with gold tassels, for example, has its virtues, modesty isn't one of them.

By surrounding ourselves with special things that we use on a daily basis, we begin to appreciate the beauty of irregular and modestly made objects—and we help others to value it, too. Thankfully, "handmade" doesn't also have to mean expensive or exclusive. While handmade goods are becoming more popular and can be very pricey (craftspeople do have to make a living), a wabi-sabi approach can be more affordable if we're discriminating about the items we truly need. But choosing to live this way is a process; it's unlikely that anyone will clear out his or her home all at once to fill it solely with wabi-sabi possessions. Instead, it's about making one decision at a time that honors the handmade. When your resources allow it, revamp your mug collection by supporting a local potter, or contribute to a skilled artisan's livelihood by finding a handmade basket for your laundry. Tap into your local art scene by finding a photographer or watercolor artist you admire and buying a print or an original piece, even if you can afford only something small. Next time you're at the farmers' market, look around for interesting items, like beeswax candles, olive-wood salad tongs, or hand-thrown flowerpots. These unique items give us a fresh appreciation for the art of making and instill a more humble appetite for the amount of *stuff* we choose to accrue.

Make Food to Nourish, Not to Impress
—

In Japanese culture, it's always appropriate to express gratitude for the meal presented to you, regardless of whether the offering is ordinary or grand. As I mentioned earlier, the widespread version of grace is to say, "I humbly receive." The Japanese excel at modest meals, but meals that also satiate. Think of rice, miso soup, ramen, curry, steamed or fried vegetables, poached fish: Even if Japanese food isn't your preference, there's no denying that these hot, hearty dishes are meant to satisfy and sustain. Everyone has his or her own version of pleasurable or consoling foods, and the most uncomplicated way to create comforting moments for guests is to nourish and warm them from the inside out.

Think of how comforting a shared cup of tea is on a bad day, or how much better a dreary evening is when you're in a cozy apartment, sharing soup and hearty bread with a circle of friends. For some, creating an artful, elaborate meal is part of the joy of having people in our homes. For others, however, the stress of wanting to impress guests through food can be a deterrent to inviting others over. Counter to what we're often taught about entertaining, wabi-sabi encourages us to make the most of very little, and to do so with joy and ease—so even if you're still learning your way around the kitchen, thoughtfully preparing a straightforward dish can be a true act of love and nourishment. One of my favorite meals in Japan was perhaps the simplest of them all: rice balls,

carefully prepared together by father, mother, and four-year-old son, something they do regularly when expecting guests. Although this meal consisted of little more than rice, it felt like a feast merely because of the way it was lovingly prepared and presented. Just as this family demonstrated to me, the more we pay attention to caring for loved ones through nourishment in all forms, the less we'll dwell on how our culinary efforts reflect upon us.

My favorite wholesome and restorative meals to make for others can usually be assembled in one pot, sometimes two. These are soups, stews, and veggie or grain bowls that typically combine vegetables, whole grains, and protein for a filling, delicious meal. These aren't always the most visually stunning dishes, but they are relatively easy to make and well suited to feeding any number of people. This is a great place to start for anyone wanting to feel more at ease in the kitchen, letting us focus on well-being rather than the wow factor. This isn't to say that comfortable cooks should stop making the delicious, beautiful dishes they love, since preparing big meals might be your own way of expressing care and attention. Whether simple or complicated, cooking as a means to nurture our guests, rather than just to present a pretty plate, allows us to fully relish the pleasure of sharing food with others.

Quit Catastrophizing

—

Japanese culture conveys an attitude of calm humility and the acceptance of whatever comes. Such a serene spirit in the face of disaster does not come easily to me: I tend to get worked up when soup boils over or I let cookies bake too long. Coming from a family of chronic apologizers (we feel responsible for anything and everything that goes wrong, even bad weather) means that I've inherited the tendency to make mountains out of molehills. A more productive mind-set would be to shake off unexpected setbacks and stop worrying about how these blunders make me look to other people. When we get hyperfocused on even minor problems, our guests feel responsible for reassuring us that everything is okay, which is hardly a fitting role. The best way around full-blown disaster is to avoid catastrophizing and to improvise with flexibility without drawing undue attention to yourself. Focusing only on your guests can ultimately lead to more creative and warmhearted entertaining for everyone.

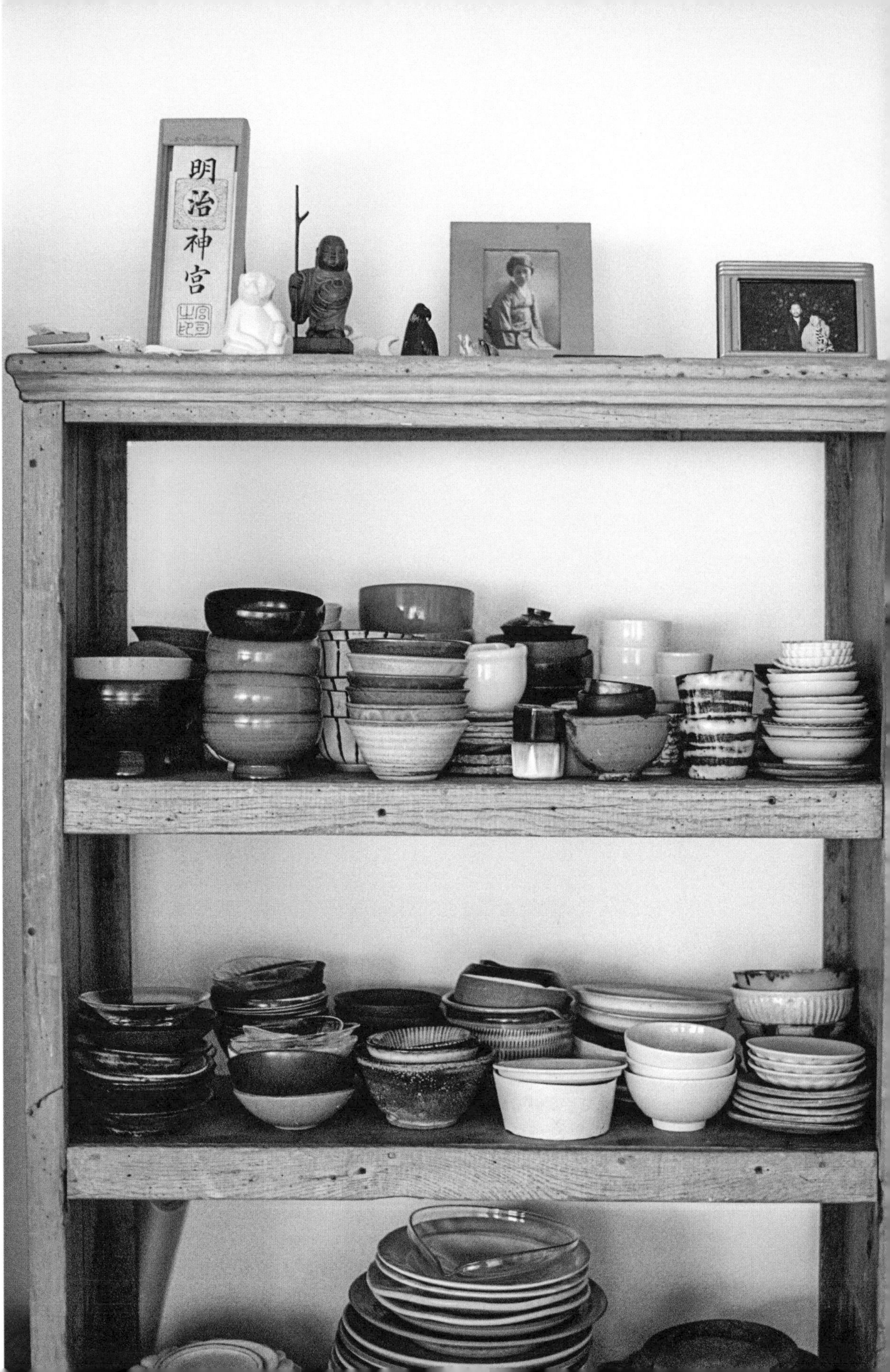
明治神宮

PRACTICAL
MATTERS

Before guests arrive, think about a handful of ways you might practice "bowing." This can be very practical, like buying a bottle of wine you know your mother-in-law loves or playing your sister's favorite album (even if you don't especially like it). Bowing is about getting yourself out of the way so you can focus on others.

—

Think of a few simple, thoughtful preparations you can take care of before people arrive, like putting a fresh bar of soap in the bathroom, having a heartfelt gift for each guest, or merely cleaning up clutter.

—

Consciously combat busyness by setting aside days to do very little. Choose *one* friend to connect with on Saturday instead of three or four, or silence your phone on Sunday so you won't be tempted to overschedule or overdose on texting and social media.

—

Next time you're in the market for something new, consider the material choice in conjunction with the pattern, price, color, practicality, and performance. Sometimes the right material can help narrow down all of these decisions! A good rule of thumb for choosing humble materials is if you can easily describe where they come from; such sources might be sheep, trees, and plants.

—

Take a wabi-sabi approach to flower arranging by going for a morning walk and collecting whatever you can find—leaves, branches, grasses, ferns, and so on. Make an arrangement that's out of your comfort zone and put it on display, even if it's just in your bedroom or in the bathroom.

Do this regularly and you'll gain more confidence (and more creativity!) when it comes to assembling inspiring combinations.

—

Coming home can become a calming ritual if you always remove your shoes and put on clogs, slippers, or sandals reserved only for indoors—and encourage others to do the same. Taking a moment to change your footwear can also help you "take off" the stresses or worries of the day.

—

Touches of the handmade can transform a house into a home, but this doesn't just include items made by skilled artisans. While homemade candles, custom furniture, and hand-stamped linen pillows are excellent additions, even just proudly displaying your child's (or your own!) ceramic sculpture, pencil drawing, or unidentifiable craft project will make your home instantly feel more intimate.

—

Develop an arsenal of wholesome recipes you can quickly draw on when you have guests—*and* that you feel confident making. It's best to know what to anticipate when cooking for friends (instead of experimenting with a new recipe for a party of ten), so devote yourself to finding a handful of easy, nourishing meals you also love making.

—

When disaster strikes, escape to the bathroom for a mini freak-out (if you must), but reenter your gathering looking cool as a cucumber. Don't let silly setbacks spoil the fun for your guests—or for yourself.

ABOVE

Both of these casual but intentional gatherings are comprised of extremely talented women with successful careers (including a chef, a florist, two food stylists, two clothing designers, and a shop owner) who still set aside time to come together and share a meal.

SETTING THE TABLE

As I've mentioned, one way to serve something straightforward and healthful to guests is to make a one-bowl meal. In Japan, a commonly used technique is to steam everything together in one special pot, called a *donabe*. I'm not experienced with this particular technique, but I have made a lot of soups and stews that follow the same principle: Just throw everything in. The three essentials are vegetables, a whole grain, and a protein of some sort. You can make a one-bowl meal look a bit more exciting by adding a garnish, whether it's cilantro, parsley, shaved cheese, sour cream (I like to use thick Greek or Icelandic yogurt as a stand-in), toasted seeds, or anything else you might fancy.

As for the rest of the table, since you have minimal tableware needs—pretty much just a bowl and a spoon—capitalize on what you *do* require and make it extra special. Give everyone a one-of-a-kind hand-thrown bowl (the thrift store is an excellent place for sourcing these), or pull out your favorite china from the cupboard; it's meant to be used, after all. Try your hand at an ikebana-inspired arrangement, and make a pot of tea to share. If you're feeling especially adventurous, serve the meal at a low table (like a coffee table) for a Japanese-style dining experience; have the diners either kneel or sit cross-legged on low cushions.

Wholesome Bowl

This is an easy go-to meal whether you're feeding yourself or a roomful of friends. I find it equally appealing for cozy evenings and hot summer nights—just sub in fresh greens like chopped kale, spinach, or arugula for your grains if you can't bring yourself to stand over the stove.

Pick your base grain, like quinoa, wild rice, lentils, couscous, or wheat berries. Follow the instructions on the box for cooking your specific grain. As a general rule, about 1 cup of uncooked grain is good for three to four people (depending on how hungry they are, of course).

In the meantime, select and prepare your vegetables. I like to use a mix of raw, colorful vegetables—cabbage, beets, carrots, red and yellow peppers, kale or spinach, broccolini, snap peas, and cauliflower—that are chopped, shredded, or grated. They can be just as tasty roasted or sautéed with a bit of olive oil and flaky sea salt (I like Maldon). Toss in some fresh herbs like dill, rosemary, or thyme if you have some on hand. You should be able to chop and sauté the vegetables while the grain is cooking, but if you plan to roast them until soft, they'll need more time to cook than your grains.

I find that including a protein keeps me feeling fuller longer; try a small piece of baked salmon or white fish, sautéed shrimp or scallops, cubed chicken or steak, tofu or tempeh, or a poached egg. Cook to your preference.

Dish the grain into a single-serving bowl and top with the veggies and protein (if using).

Unify all of the ingredients with a sauce. Maybe your preference is salsa, sriracha, peanut sauce, yellow curry, soy sauce, tahini, or a tasty mix of olive oil and lemon juice. Garnish with your preferred toppings, such as chopped scallions, toasted or black sesame seeds, or avocado slices.

Simple Traditional Noodles

One of my favorite meals in Japan was a relaxed summer lunch served to us at chef Yuri Nomura's home. Its beautiful presentation was made even more impressive by how simple but nourishing the ingredients were. The meal consisted of noodles, broth, and a variety of choose-your-own-ingredients to add to it. This is a lovely dish for summer, when the noodles are traditionally eaten cold, using the broth as a dipping sauce, but it can be a comforting, customizable meal for any time of year.

To serve as a soup: If you have the time, make your own vegetable, chicken, or beef broth from scratch. Otherwise, choose your favorite premade broth and season as you like. Heat as directed, portioning out about 2 cups per person.

For the noodles, use any kind you'd like and cook according to package instructions and serving size. For a more authentic Japanese approach, use soba (buckwheat noodles).

Next, prepare vegetables and/or protein that can be added to the broth: chopped green onion, pickled red onion, sliced cucumbers, chopped cilantro, cubed chicken or tofu, smoked fish—the options are limitless.

Serve the broth, the noodles, and the rest of the ingredients separately, so that each guest can customize his or her own bowl.

To serve cold: Chill the broth, or find a recipe for *tsuyu* dipping sauce, which is the traditional Japanese way of eating this dish. For the noodles, cook as directed and, after straining them, cover with two or three ice cubes to cool them down quickly. Instead of soba noodles, you may want to try *somen*, which are thinner than soba and made of wheat rather than buckwheat. Again, leave any accompaniments separate for guests to customize their bowls. This includes the noodles, as this dish is traditionally eaten by quickly dunking the chilled noodles into the broth/dipping sauce before each bite.

O-nigiri (Rice Balls)

Rice balls are a staple in the Japanese diet for many reasons—they are simple to make, a filling snack, a great addition to any meal, and easy to take on the go.

Rice balls can be made with fillings like salmon, curried chicken, or steamed veggies, or they can be made with just a topping like sesame seeds or umeboshi—which are pickled plums (as seen here).

Allow for 1 cup of uncooked Japanese sushi rice per person. For four servings, start with 4 cups of rice, which will make 2 rice balls per person. Rinse the rice in a mesh strainer until the water runs clear. Then pour the rice into a saucepan with 4½ cups of water and cook according to the instructions on the package.

Once the rice is done resting (about 10 minutes), add 1 cup white vinegar and 2 tablespoons sugar to the cooked rice.

In a separate bowl, combine 1 cup of water and about ¼ teaspoon salt for wetting your hands before handling the rice. Separate the rice into eight equal portions, about ½ cup for each ball.

If you're adding a filling, halve each of the eight portions, create a dimple in the center of each half, and stuff with a small amount of vegetables, fish, or whatever filling you are using. Join the two halves of rice back together, and form into a small ball. Either wrap each portion of rice with a ½-inch strip of nori or serve strips separately so that the balls can be picked up more easily and fingers stay rice-free. Sprinkle with sesame seeds or any other desired toppings.

Chapter Two

DENMARK

AS SIMPLE AS POSSIBLE, NOT ONE BIT MORE

The Danish are known for perfect simplicity; they've long been producing utilitarian, unadorned designs, and they rarely own more than they need. Perhaps this sense of sparseness is inspired by the flat, open landscape of Denmark, which is mostly composed of green farmland and sandy coastline. And yet, this somewhat spartan lifestyle doesn't prevent the Danes from also excelling at great warmth and coziness. Glowing candles, woodstoves, and intimate seating like benches and small tables can be found at cafés and in homes of any size or style, whether centuries-old farmhouses or modern, updated flats. The Danish word *hygge* embodies this cozy approach to hospitality, which is all about making guests feel completely content in any setting.

I've experienced the sensation of hygge in many places, but it was the Danes who gave me a word to express it and who have persuaded me that it should be a model for entertaining. Like wabi-sabi, hygge is hard to translate into just a word or two; it refers to the way something looks and feels, but it's also a way of life. Some define it as "the art of creating intimacy," because, simply put, it's about creating spaces that encourage a sense of camaraderie, using humble components, and finding the joy in ordinary moments. Hygge is a feeling of warmth instilled by our environment, but also something we can encourage within ourselves by learning to be present. The Danes are masters at cultivating hygge in their everyday routines. Hygge can be found in hot chocolate and warm cookies on a snowy evening, or a sunset picnic with grilled fish and big slices of watermelon during the warm seasons.

This inclination toward creating warmhearted experiences—and taking the time to enjoy them—is likely the reason that Denmark always lands so high on the happiness scale year after year. Intentionally trying to infuse hygge into our lives inspires us to slow down, and reminds us to savor even the simplest of settings.

During several visits to Denmark over the years, I've witnessed this kind of hospitality in many forms: I recall a low-key children's birthday party turned magical through the simple act of hanging a couple of ropes between trees to make a tightrope of sorts, keeping both kids and adults happy for a long time. I've seen a simple Sunday family dinner transform into a feast with the addition of a few guests, a gigantic loaf of bread, and some more side dishes to accommodate the extra mouths. Neither of these occasions required an exceptional setting or fancy food to make a special memory. Rather, they embodied the kind of uncomplicated pleasures that remind us that we can kindle joy with the most common, essential elements. Denmark has given me plenty of ideas for simultaneously finding simplicity and delight in my home; the following ideas may help you find them in yours, too.

The Simple Host
Commit to Coffee Breaks

—

Drinking coffee with friends is nearly sacred in Denmark—it might even be considered the equivalent of the tea ceremony in Japan. Both rituals celebrate being present in the moment and stepping away from anything else for that period of time. Scandinavians in general regularly take time for warm drinks and treats, usually favoring something much slower and more social than caffeine to go. While the Danish don't assign a proper name to it (in Sweden it's referred to as *fika*), breaking from work or Saturday chores to enjoy a cup of coffee with a friend is seen as a priority rather than a luxury.

Much of my personal experience in Denmark came during my early twenties, when I worked on two organic farms in the Danish countryside. The majority of my time was spent on a berry farm on a tiny island with two hundred inhabitants, where I lived with the farmer and his family. In the midst of even the busiest jam-making days, the farmer insisted that we all take a mid-morning coffee break, and sometimes an afternoon one, too. On damp, drizzly mornings and

sunny days alike, we sat around a makeshift table in the yard and shared a strong pot of coffee. Those gatherings stand out in my memory as significant moments of camaraderie and happiness, set apart from the relative intensity of the workday.

These coffee breaks don't have to be premeditated (no homemade baked goods necessary) to provide an undistracted pause. Commit to taking a "time-out" at least a few times a week (if not more), but let these breathers happen spontaneously. If you spot a neighbor while out getting the mail, invite him or her in for a cup of coffee or tea and a simple treat, like a tangerine or whatever you may have on hand. Or leave Sunday afternoons open for having a friend over on the spur of the moment—maybe someone you've had on your mind or haven't seen in a while. It's the simplicity of these times that makes them special, offering an opportunity to be wholeheartedly present for the moment right in front of us.

Make Hosting a Habit

—

Making a habit of opening our doors to friends and family keeps us feeling connected, and refines our idea of what entertaining requires. It's common in Denmark to invite others over for meals, and it's generally understood that being warm and snug at home is one of life's greatest joys (the long months of dark winter days and frigid weather undoubtedly contribute to this feeling). The limited population of the small country creates an intimate, family-centered culture, and many families keep alive a tradition of weekly meals long after kids reach adulthood and have their own children.

But habitual hosting isn't reserved only for family members or special occasions; gathering regularly helps develop a sense of community and familiarity between just about anyone. During the years I was planning events professionally, my life involved more hosting than ever before, and frequent get-togethers in my home or backyard became the norm. Sometimes these occasions were casual, last-minute dinners, and other times they were regularly scheduled gatherings, like a book club or a weekly catch-up with a close friend. In each case, I found that the more often I welcomed the same people into my home, the more connected I felt, and the less intimidating it became to invite people over on a whim. I also discovered that a gathering can revolve around little more than well-seasoned popcorn and a bottle of wine, or a bowl of fresh strawberries and glasses of sparkling water. As hosting became a habit, I started to feel freer asking people to contribute dishes for potlucks, and worried less about the baseboards being dusted or the cobwebs being swept away before making plans. In the process, entertaining became simpler and more enjoyable, and I felt happier and more rooted to the place and people I surrounded myself with. I learned that when we allow entertaining to become a part of everyday life, our experiences together can be more beautifully uncomplicated and rich.

OPPOSITE

Mikkel Karstad is a talented and highly sought after chef in Copenhagen, but he also cooks phenomenally for his family, which includes his wife, Camilla, and their four children. Mikkel and Camilla are gracious hosts, quick to offer an invitation to their home and willing to share whatever they have. Here, Mikkel prepares to make grilled squid for an extended family dinner.

Clear Clutter

—

The Danes celebrate stripped-back purity all the time. If you want proof, look no further than Danish furniture: the famously minimal but functional pieces tend to be clean, wooden, and modest. Their lack of frills or fanfare makes them timeless and elegant, allowing them to stand happily on their own. While I'm not suggesting you go out and buy a truckload of Danish furniture, you can apply this same principle to each room in your house. For example, a Danish couple I know pared down their bedroom to only a low-profile bed covered in a fluffy white duvet. No bookshelves, no piles of clothes, nothing on the walls; just the bed. For two very busy adults with active careers and a handful of young children, this private room is reserved for rest, relaxation, and connecting with each other—and only that. You might imagine, as I initially did, that the space feels empty, but it instead feels like a sanctuary, set apart from the rest of the house. Sticking to just the basics means there's nothing to encourage distraction in a room intended for quiet and togetherness.

That lack of distraction can hold true for any-place where we gather, whether it's the kitchen, living room, dining room, or patio. While certain decor can create a pleasant diversion, clutter detracts from whatever calm our homes provide. Your version of clutter may be piles of old catalogs, trinkets you no longer want, remote controls that don't work, an attic stuffed with "just in case" items, boxes of projects saved for later . . . you get the idea. Even if the offending objects aren't visible, they create a mental and physical block to living simply. The ongoing goal of a wabi-sabi mind-set is to become increasingly unencumbered, whether that means donating clothes you haven't worn in years or clearing the emotional clutter of nostalgic items it's time to let go of. The ultimate purpose of decluttering is to make our homes as comforting and carefree as possible, for both ourselves and whomever we entertain.

The Simple Home
Collect, Then Curate
—

"Pare down to the essence, but don't remove the poetry." This lovely motto comes from Leonard Koren's book *Wabi-Sabi for Artists, Designers, Poets & Philosophers*, and to me it sums up the Danish philosophy of seeking simplicity without sacrificing beauty. This mind-set helps refresh our perspective when our homes begin to fill up with too much stuff and we're overwhelmed instead of enlivened by our possessions. It's easy to understand why so many of us are prone to collect—it's fun! There's pleasure in combing flea markets, shops, and online stores for just the right addition, and this impulse can become especially addictive when we're building prized collections of dishware, blankets, shoes, magazines, plants, shells, candles, pottery, pillows, knickknacks, baskets, framed art . . . well, you fill in the blanks. Our homes should inspire and rejuvenate us, but if every nook and cranny is crammed with belongings, there's little space left for the imagination or for relaxation. The excitement of collecting should (ideally, at least) be balanced by a willingness to edit and refine, since having fewer possessions makes each one more cherished—and in my eyes, that's where the "poetry" part comes in.

I've found plenty of poetry in Denmark, where I've fallen in love with Danish design and also been challenged to reevaluate what's necessary. Carefully considered homes have shown me that drawing attention to a single item can be more striking than showcasing everything you own in one setting—say, for example, displaying all your favorite art on one wall or overcrowding a shelf with stacks of books. Instead, that chosen item might be a finely woven rattan chair in the corner, a straw hat above the bed, a distinctive vase on a credenza, or a solo black-and-white photograph. Letting beautiful things speak for themselves can be a graceful statement, and minimal decor creates a sense of ease and brightness both in daily life and while we entertain. If you simply can't seem to let go of some items, put them in the basement or attic for a while and see if your mind comes back to these collected objects at any point. If you haven't found yourself missing them after a few months, it's probably appropriate to pass them on to another collector. Learning to prune our belongings makes our homes—and the people within them—flourish more fully.

Let Home Be Homey

—

It may sound obvious to say that of all the places we spend our time, home should be the homiest, but by that I mean warm, welcoming, personal, and intimate. An important part of homeyness is offering a safe haven to whoever might enter and providing comfort, calm, and shelter from the world. The best sanctuaries are free from stiffness and the need for proper posture at the dinner table; from worry about leaving windows and doors open; from fear of using the wrong fork or sitting in a forbidden chair. Instead, homeyness is soft beds and couches we want to curl into, quiet corners in which to sit and read together, and a feeling of seclusion and contentment that allows us to come out of our shells. Creating a homey space is a way of practicing hygge—it's learning to focus on comfort and ease rather than overly polished design or what looks "cool" at the expense of making us feel truly at home.

The spaces I have loved the most and felt most relaxed in have always lacked grandeur or luxurious details. Rather, they are small but serene rooms, private nooks in which to hide away, with a satisfying scent, unassuming but comfortable furniture, plenty of fresh air, and a feeling of cleanliness without being sterile. Above all, these places give me permission to be myself; to sprawl across an armchair, flip through a magazine on the floor, or eat a snack in the living room without fear of getting into trouble. I remember once being scolded at someone's home for lying on a white bedspread (on the bed I was sleeping in, no less) because it might get dirty, and I was told to remove it before I lounged there. The experience confirmed for me that while home is many different things, it shouldn't be a museum. Letting your home be homey means that it's lived in and loved, that things are used for their proper purpose, and that you, your children, and your guests don't have to tiptoe around, worrying about spoiling your possessions. A perfectly imperfect space will be filled with personality and the remnants of real life, whether that's dog hair on the bed, scuff marks on the floor, or a tear in your favorite quilt. Spills, rips, stains, nicks, and nail holes are signs of life! Instead of getting worked up about these minor flaws, consider them evidence of truly being at home. Homeyness lets us embrace home as our refuge and retreat and a place to be entirely ourselves—and to let our company do the same.

Let Beauty and Utility Overlap
—

Being beautiful should go perfectly hand in hand with being useful; just as a nice appearance shouldn't be more important than functionality, an object with a clear purpose doesn't have to be unsightly, either. Danish design has always excelled at combining beauty and utility: as the refined, iconic Vipp trash can that designer Holger Nielsen originally made in 1939 for his wife's hair salon (and which is now seen in homes around the world) proved, even throwing out garbage can be pleasurable. Wabi-sabi promotes a similarly resourceful approach by encouraging us to live with useful things we love and make home life function with as few things as possible. Investing in beautiful utilitarian objects simplifies our spaces because we end up needing fewer things to help us *and* make us happy.

Living in a small house with almost no built-in storage, I am mindful about every purchase, especially since there's very little room to hide anything that's unattractive. Over time I've tried to gather eye-pleasing, well-designed objects that also assist me in my daily life, like baskets that store blankets, electronics, or books, and a wood-handled dustpan and broom I don't mind people seeing. The open shelving in my kitchen means that I use glass storage for nonperishables like pasta, popcorn, and dried beans, and wood-slatted crates for less compelling necessities like aluminum foil and parchment paper. A collection of favorite towels is stacked on bathroom wall shelves, and an unassuming but nice-looking laundry bag keeps dirty clothes out of sight. Even my leaky copper watering can gives me a momentary spark of delight when I see its evolving patina and long, slim spout. The fact that these kinds of ordinary objects are necessary for everyday life only makes me more certain that we should also be able to find pleasure in seeing and using them on a daily basis.

The Simple Table

Leave Room for Unexpected Beauty

—

Sometimes the most satisfying solution in home decorating or entertaining is the one that's most surprising. That's particularly true for the table, where we tend to rely too much on conventional aesthetics. With so many options at our disposal, the tabletop can quickly become a hodgepodge of colored, patterned, and textured linens; candles and candlesticks; floral arrangements; glassware; silverware; and countless other extraneous bits of decor. So when you get the impulse to exhibit every dining-related thing you own, take a step back and reconsider how you can strip away instead of heap on. If we intentionally create bare space, there's more room for unexpected beauty—and imagination. Instead of settling for a ho-hum bouquet, for example, go outside and really look around at what's there. Take a yard clipping even if it's just a bit of green, or, if you don't have a yard or trees on your street, check out the fridge. A bowl of persimmons, Meyer lemons, or blood oranges can be a striking centerpiece; you can also skip the bowl entirely and set a few pears right on the table. Even a vase of leafy greens or leeks can work beautifully.

The food we serve can be decor all on its own—just picture sliced purple radishes, pink pickled eggs (use beet juice for a radical color), deep ruby pomegranates, orangey aged Gouda, or a pale peach papaya. This kind of edible tableau works particularly well when it has little visual competition, so set the table with only the pieces of flatware you really need, and omit your usual place mats. Making space from the get-go always allows us to discover something inspiring—and delightfully unplanned— along the way.

DENMARK

Make Seasonal Smørrebrød

—

Smørrebrød might be considered the national dish of Denmark. The term, which simply means "butter and bread" in Danish, refers to open-face sandwiches built on a foundation of dense rye bread, slathered with something (like butter), and covered with toppings to your heart's delight. Traditional Danish combinations include ingredients such as smoked or pickled fish, seafood, thinly sliced boiled eggs, red onions, cucumbers, cold cuts, cheese, and fresh herbs like dill. Whether you're hosting a laid-back Saturday lunch or an Easter feast, a beautiful way to simplify any occasion is to make a smorgasbord of ingredients that you can customize to your tastes and the season, and that guests can in turn choose for themselves. It's also relatively effortless: As the host, all you have to do is get creative in displaying the smørrebrød's components; the rest is up to them.

Because the Danish have smørrebrød down to an art, I'm certain that the first time I was introduced to this lunchtime custom, I both prepared and ate my smørrebrød the "wrong" way, pairing my bread choice and fish improperly and adding my toppings in an unusual order, but outside of Denmark, I think it's acceptable to take liberties. My suggestion is to use this Danish tradition simply as a framework for creating something uniquely yours, something a little more wabi-sabi. Each half-slice or triangle of bread is an opportunity to layer and pair new, interesting combinations, and each guest gets to create something to his or her own liking. In late summer, try goat cheese and quartered fresh figs; or in spring, experiment with a pea-and-mint puree topped by grated Parmesan. The options are nearly limitless, and as with all things wabi-sabi, combining even the plainest, earthiest elements can produce something truly lovely—and, in this case, completely delicious.

PRACTICAL MATTERS

Give yourself permission to step away from to-do lists and work tasks on a regular basis. Whether it's coffee, tea, cookies, or a midmorning banana that you drop everything for, sharing this little respite with a pal makes it that much easier to take a quick mental retreat.

—

Dedicate one night per week to hosting—whether that means making a simple meal for you and a friend (or even just you and your spouse!), or holding a weekly meeting of friends to discuss a book, parenting, creative projects, or whatever topic gets you most excited.

—

Commit to memory a few go-to, super-simple recipes for breakfast, lunch, and dinner (or good fallbacks like prepared food from the grocery store when life's too busy); doing so makes hosting casual last-minute get-togethers a cinch.

—

Be conscious about how much you let accrue on the coffee table, on the kitchen counter, or in the closet. Ask yourself if you really need to keep those ten extra magazines, or if you honestly think you'll ever wear that fringed tank top again.

—

Look at your home with the eye of an editor or a curator—instead of trying to fit as much as possible into a space, consider how you might pare down and simplify. If you have ten special items on your bureau, select your five favorites and keep only those. Put away the others for another day when you feel like mixing things up, or get rid of them altogether.

—

Make cozy zones in your home—snug little nooks that people can't help but cuddle up in. Blankets or throws, soft pillows (forget any that are uncomfortably stiff or have a rough, scratchy texture), rugs, and books or magazines are perfect additions to these spaces.

—

Be more discriminating when it comes to household purchases. Instead of always opting for what's cheap and convenient, try to find durable items that are useful and beautiful at the same time. Doing so makes more room for things we keep just because they make us happy.

—

Consider your table an artist's canvas—focus on leaving enough negative space (the areas that remain empty) to really draw attention to those unexpected bits of beauty, like a vibrant salad, a casual backyard bouquet, or glasses of subtly blush-colored rosé.

—

Don't just think about your menu in terms of flavors; consider a variety of colors and textures, too. Liven up a simple roasted veggie recipe by selecting vibrant yellow and red carrots, green or purple cauliflower, striped beets, or pink and white radishes.

—

Take an unconventional approach when it comes to sandwich options. Throw in some fruit (like pear or apple slices), soft cheeses (like Brie, goat, or some variety of blue), and pretty things to pile on top, like edible flowers, shredded basil, or sprouts.

SETTING THE TABLE

As with everything Danish, setting the table should be simple through and through, including the meal, decor, and necessities like plates and napkins. A common spread might include grilled fish, a side of roasted potatoes (a Danish necessity), a loaf of bread, and a fennel salad. To decorate in the same vein, lay the aromatic tips of spruce branches (or something similar) in the center of the table instead of flowers. As for tableware and glassware, choose something clean and unadorned for a true Scandinavian look—simple plates, no-frills flatware, sturdy glasses. Some of my favorite tabletop treasures (found in a Danish thrift store) are small rectangular half-inch-thick wooden boards made for eating toast or open-face sandwiches; basically, little handheld cutting boards for each diner. While these likely won't hold an entire dinner meal (unless you eat like a mouse), they're perfectly lovely for a bit of bread and butter on the side. For a thoroughly Danish meal, top off the table with a round of beer!

Smørrebrød

For a casual, Danish-inspired meal, start with smørrebrød as the foundation and build from there. As noted earlier in this chapter, smørrebrød are open-faced sandwiches traditionally built on a thin slice of buttered rye bread. An easy way to approach these is to simply buy a variety of ingredients that your guests can personalize into their own creations. Side dishes might include a cabbage salad, a variety of pickled items that could double as smørrebrød toppings (like pickled beets, pickled cucumbers, or pickled figs), and a cold potato salad chock-full of fresh herbs.

Start with a dense bread like rye—or try pumpernickel, thin focaccia, or even a halved bagel. Toppings might include the following:

— Fresh and smoked fish

— Deli meats, like turkey, ham, or salami slices

— Pâté

— Fresh vegetables

— Pickled vegetables

— Hard-boiled-egg slices

— A variety of spreads, like butter, mayonnaise, mustard, whipped or creamy cheeses, and smashed avocado

— Garnish-type toppings, like sprouts, edible flowers, pea shoots, and shredded or chopped herbs

Or think outside the box and come up with some of your own unique combinations for layering on top!

Æbleflæsk

A popular Danish dish is æbleflæsk, *which means "apple pork";
I remember devouring this yummy mixture with toast on a cold
island morning before heading out to paint a barn in the rain, but
it's the kind of dish that can be enjoyed with breakfast, lunch, or
dinner or as a midday snack. Basically, it's sautéed apples with
bacon, onions, and a bit of herbs (like sage or thyme) with sugar,
honey, or maple syrup mixed in. This can be eaten as a side dish
by itself or slathered on bread.*

Begin by frying a few pieces of bacon (about one slice per two
apples); you can either leave it in strips or chop it into smaller
pieces. Fry the bacon until it is slightly soft, not too crispy.

Meanwhile, peel and chop a white or sweet yellow onion. This
is optional, but it adds bulk to the dish in a nice way. Next, chop
some apples (about one apple per person since they will cook
down) into either thin slices or dice—whatever your preference.
I like leaving the peel on, but it can be removed if desired.

Take the bacon out of the pan and place it on a paper towel to
absorb some of the grease, but leave the remaining grease in the
pan to cook the onions and apples.

Lightly sauté the onions until golden and translucent, then
add the apples. At this point, I throw in something sweet *and*
savory to the dish; for four apples, add about 2 teaspoons of
your desired sweetener and a tablespoon of fresh herbs, such as
thyme leaves. Place a lid over the pan so that everything steams
together. Cook until soft, around 15 minutes.

Finish by mixing in the bacon and adding a dash of salt.

Baked Apples

*Baked apples are an easy and (potentially) healthful treat for chil-
dren and adults alike. Use one apple per guest, and dig out the
core without going all the way through to the bottom. The apple
filling can be as simple as chopped nuts (I like pecans or walnuts)
and a little honey, or you can dress it up with oats, brown sugar
(as an alternative to the honey), a bit of butter, and warm spices
like cinnamon and nutmeg.*

Fill a baking dish with ¾ to 1 cup of water (just enough to cover
the bottom), cover the apples with tinfoil or a baking dish lid,
and bake at 375°F until they're soft—start with a bake time of
25 minutes and check periodically thereafter. If desired, you
can bake them uncovered for the last 10 minutes for a more
caramelized result.

For utter deliciousness, serve the apples with crème fraîche
that's been whipped with a bit of vanilla extract and maple
syrup to taste.

1
1
3

BEING CLOSE
BRINGS COMFORT

Invite Openness and Belonging
Through Intimate Spaces

Growing up on the central coast of California has convinced me that warm, Mediterranean climates help us get close and let loose—sharing a blanket at the beach or lounging in a backyard hammock with a friend is the kind of situation that enables me to be myself and open up. Likewise, when we gather with just a few people, tucking in around a small table, sitting shoulder to shoulder on a bench, or eating picnic-style, we feel more connected to one another.

These intimate wabi-sabi spaces, which are by nature small and private, encourage us to sit close and interact more naturally. When we let comfort and closeness be our guides to hosting, all of our decisions become simpler and more carefree.

Whether it's a party of two or twenty-five, experience has shown me that people become comfortable when they are relaxed, welcome, and content, and being in cozy, low-key, personal places enhances those feelings. When you invite friends over, opt for a snug space to gather in. Eat in the tiny breakfast nook instead of the formal dining room, or bring dinner onto your laps on the porch. Drag a small table into the garden and eat surrounded by flowers and weeds. If you're an apartment-dweller, invite others over for gatherings on the stoop, the rooftop, or even the fire escape. Moments shared in unconventional places make for more interesting memories and, I believe, more lasting connections.

Here are some elements of California living that have shown me how to encourage a spirit of openness and a sense of belonging among my guests on any occasion. I'm certain they can do the same for you.

OPPOSITE

Andrew and Carissa Gallo, along with their children, Rinah and River, regularly open their doors for casual, intimate gatherings at their Laurel Canyon home.

CALIFORNIA

PREVIOUS PAGES

Joya Rose Groves, an illustrator living on the edge of an idyllic little town called Summerland, is the epitome of the kind and candid host. Here, she welcomes friends for a prework breakfast gathering of biscuits and coffee.

The Intimate Host
Be Kind and Candid
—

We've all crafted a way of portraying ourselves in public, filtering our words so we don't reveal too much about ourselves, and trying to say the perfect thing to leave the right impression. But I've found that being candid, as hard as it is, is much more rewarding. It's about being vulnerable and letting people into your life even when it feels inconvenient or messy. Those days when you're exhausted, furious at your boss, or feeling let down by your spouse are the ones when you most need a friend. Not a text, not even a phone call, but a real live friend to commiserate with and to console you.

Being candid also goes hand in hand with being kind. Kindness is listening more than talking, acting gently, and being considerate of others' feelings. Showing hospitality lets us practice empathy in super-practical ways, like inviting a friend who's lost someone to come over for a big pot of soup, and sending him home with leftovers. Or making time to see a loved one for breakfast before work when you know she's having a tough week. The joy of no-strings-attached kindness can be just as gratifying for you as it is for your guests, and it makes hosting feel more like a privilege than a chore.

Interacting so openly and directly can seem a little overwhelming at first, but I think the best way to begin is to ask questions and not be afraid to share yourself. *How are your parents doing? What was challenging at work (or with your kids) this week? What's something you're looking forward to this month? How are you adjusting to being married/being single/being a parent/having a new job?* Simple, heartfelt questions can go a long way, and you'll be surprised at how much closer you'll feel to the people around you when you ask them—and answer them yourself.

Congregate in the Kitchen

—

In most cultures, the kitchen was once a part of the house that guests wouldn't enter, let alone flock to while food was being prepared. In some parts of the world, like China and regions of South America, it's still off-limits for company that isn't family. For many of us, however, the kitchen is one of the coziest spaces in our home, a place we gravitate to because it's where the action is. The vibrant smells, tastes, sounds, and colors of the kitchen draw us close together. Standing over the stove or sink inspires casual conversation, and letting guests share in the preparation—even if they're just the designated taste-testers—makes the enjoyment of the food that much richer.

I learned to cook in various California homes by observation and then through trial and error, so for me the kitchen conjures up memories of fresh, fragrant rosemary and cilantro; the scent of citrus; open windows; a place to chat and gather; stacks of cookbooks; and something roasting or baking in the oven. In contrast, for many years I lived in a studio apartment with a kitchen the size of a small walk-in closet. It was not an easy space to make meals in, let alone leave room for others to join me. Even so, during parties, book club meetings, or casual dinners, it was inevitably where people wanted to hang out. I didn't understand why they'd want to cram into this tiny space with me while I banged cupboards and clanged pots, but the proportions actually created the perfect-size space for close, comfortable encounters.

Beyond just providing a low-key place to gather, welcoming guests into the kitchen forces you to be okay with letting people see your mess. This means your company might see piles of eggshells in the sink, potato skins on the counter, or dried red lentils spilled all over the floor. Allowing friends, family, or even new acquaintances to enter this space in spite of minor chaos encourages a sense of immediate transparency. The intimacy of wabi-sabi requires relatability. There's relief in knowing that the people we spend time with have cooking disasters once in a while, too. It's by allowing familiarity in these ordinary moments that we feel most closely tied to our company.

Use Touch to Welcome and Comfort

—

It's no surprise that warm, sunny spots generally encourage more friendly touch than places with long, cold winters. In California we bare our skin almost year-round, instantly making a hug, a high five, or a shoulder squeeze both more casual and more direct. But whether you are a warm- or cold-climate dweller, everyone needs to experience personal touch—it ties us to friends and loved ones in ways that little else can.

When we entertain, we set the tone for how company feels in our presence—whether close and comfortable or distant and tense. Touch allows us to communicate emotions in subtle, meaningful ways that language sometimes can't. Using our bodies may be the best way to offer empathy to a grieving friend, or to celebrate a big accomplishment and a happy occasion. An excited hug or a kiss on the cheek can be a more powerful way to express something than actually saying it out loud. Similarly, sitting on the couch and holding a friend's hand or rubbing his or her back in silence may be just what's needed.

We all benefit from comforting touch, but it takes the right setting for it to happen spontaneously. It's easier to have intimate encounters when we're sitting on a narrow porch or huddled around an outdoor fire than if we're spread out at a formal dining table. Playing host means choosing the right environment to match the occasion and the comfort level of your guests. When in doubt, pick a place where you feel most at ease being yourself, and you'll discover that showing you care by getting cozy comes quite naturally.

What you can't see in this photo is that while preparing to put our kebabs on the grill for this beach picnic, I tripped and sent the majority of our dinner-to-be flying into the sand. I had to heed my own advice in this particular moment and remember not to sweat it. Naturally, we made do and still had a great time—right along with some sandy salmon.

Don't Sweat the Small Stuff

—

Coastal Californians excel at hanging loose. I think it's a combination of the weather, the water, and the warmth that instills this knack for slowed-down, chilled-out living. While we can't all enjoy year-round beach-lounging weather, there is something of this spirit that I think anyone can learn to embody. At its heart is the belief that everything is going to work out in the end— there's no point in getting hung up on details that are inconsequential to the big picture.

In wabi-sabi terms, this mode of living is what might be called *acceptance of the inevitable*. This describes a world perspective that accepts that people and things have flaws and will fade. It not only allows for imperfection but actually embraces it. It means saying to yourself, *Whatever will be, will be. Calm down and mellow out*.

Having a laid-back spirit doesn't merely help *you* to enjoy yourself more fully, it lets your guests relax, too. More often than not when guests appear at my door, I am still sweating in the kitchen, buzzing around in a minor panic trying to pull everything together. The simpler, more wabi-sabi approach would be to Zen out, so to speak, and to let things unfold naturally. But what if the cake is inedible and the toilet is overflowing? Zenning out in this moment is extremely difficult. The only reasonable thing to do is to give yourself some grace and remember that these things happen. Maybe this means eating half an hour later than you planned to or picking up Thai food to replace the chicken you accidentally burned to a crisp. In the long run, these kinds of trivial setbacks or changes in plans amount to very little indeed. Laugh when you want to cry and soon others will be laughing, too.

The Intimate Home
Introduce Nature to Create Calm

—

Natural beauty abounds in California. The state boasts the Pacific coastline, cacti-filled deserts, the Sierra Nevada, and countless other wonders. Each of these landscapes inspires a sense of serenity and awe through muted colors, vast expanses, and airy openness. I love stepping into homes that echo these same attributes—I immediately feel quieted, just like when I stand at the ocean's edge. What is it about these spaces that gives me a sense of contentment? Well, it's many things; chief among them is the careful use of color drawn from tones found only in the natural world. Wabi-sabi manifests in heavier shades, like the dark grays, blues, greens, and rusts found in the sea and in trees like olive and sequoia, and in lighter hues that stick to the realm of muted pastels, like you might see on the desert floor, in beach grasses, or in the bark of a eucalyptus tree.

These homes also provide a feeling of breathability. There's a delicate balance between the empty places and the *stuff*—spaces left bare on walls and on floors, on tabletops and counters, even on beds or couches (forget the giant mound of pillows!). Fresh air moves freely through open windows, which also let in soft, filtered light. It's the sensation of a room that's been edited to the essentials without seeming stark or appearing neglected. This ability to refine is the heart of wabi-sabi.

However, to be essential doesn't mean that an object is strictly *useful* in the normal sense of the word. Instead, an object's utility might be that it gives you a sense of tranquillity when you look at it. Think an abstract watercolor, ivy vines in the bathroom, or a pile of inspirational books. To this end, creating calm isn't merely about *mimicking* nature, it's also about *introducing* nature into your home. It's finding beauty in insignificant, often-overlooked objects like blue-fringed feathers or half-broken shells. It's mounting strangely shaped driftwood on the wall, putting tangled tumbleweeds in a corner, or setting a pile of smooth gray beach stones on the mantel.

Wabi-sabi suggests that your own version of peacefulness will always be personal, intuitive, and idiosyncratic. That being said, wabi-sabi *does* represent a particular sensitivity and a way of doing things. It's in the colors, material choices, shapes, smells, and sounds we include in our homes. I've found that the more intimate and personal I make my surroundings, the more universally appealing they seem to be to others. It always amazes me that the bizarre things I find delightful and soothing—a single fern frond in a tall vase; the scent of orange blossoms diffused in the air; or old, speckled pottery full of fossils and dried plant life—can have this comforting effect on other people, too. Arranging our spaces to reflect the unique beauty of the natural world always creates a little room to stop and pause.

FOLLOWING PAGES
These quiet, nature-inspired scenes were found around Wanda Weller's Ojai home. The lovely landscape painting was done by Wanda's friend John Rapp, a local artist.

NATURE'S
COLOR PALETTE

CALIFORNIA

Leave the Door Unlocked

—

One of the things I value greatly about my California childhood is that our house doors were nearly always kept unlocked. My parents freely welcomed friends, family, and strangers into our home without any fear or trepidation. This instilled in me an attitude of trust and freedom toward the outside world. Obviously in many places it wouldn't be safe or sensible to live this way, but I've realized that this simple detail from my past sets my perspective apart from that of many people I know.

A wabi-sabi spirit adopts this same attitude; whether you literally leave the door open is up to you. When you start picturing your home as a refuge for others, it allows whatever you offer to be a gift rather than a burden. It's about sharing your physical possessions, grand or simple as they may be, but also freely sharing yourself. Your home reveals your tastes, your interests, and a private version of you. For some, this kind of vulnerability is a relief from the superficial encounters we often experience at work, for example. For others, the idea of letting people see us for who we truly are might seem terrifying. It can be a challenge for anyone to sit back while guests riffle through carefully stacked piles, endanger treasured objects, or spill red wine on the white couch. This is when my most anti-wabi-sabi tendencies kick in and I have to take some deep breaths. I frequently have to remind myself that hosting teaches me to let go; it's an opportunity to share what I have—even when this means things get broken or stained. These moments help me to loosen up and accept the inevitable. Things don't last forever, and too much attachment to them only leaves us disappointed.

Beginning small is a good way to test the waters when it comes to inviting people over. Small groups of two or three make for super-relaxed interactions, and will help you warm up to entertaining. The point is not the quantity of guests but the quality of your interactions. Maybe it's fresh bagels or biscuits on a weekend morning before hitting the farmers' market together, a pizza dinner on the porch, or even just a cup of coffee shared on the stoop. The important thing is not to overthink it but to willingly offer whatever's personal to you (time, space, belongings, efforts in the kitchen), however minimal or modest you may consider it. Once we open our doors even a few times, we begin to see that welcoming people into our homes and lives can be extremely rewarding.

Personalize with the Particular

—

Five things we're grateful for every night at dinner. I was a guest in a well-known interior designer's home and found this scribbled reminder taped to the hutch by the dining room table, acting as a visual prompt for a daily dinner activity. How quickly this little piece of evidence showed what was important to this family! The straightforward particularity of the note revealed that gratitude was high on their list of values. This kind of simple expression is key to making your space feel warm and personal. The more *you* your house is, the more easily your guests will understand what you care about.

I feel least at home in places that lack personal touches, traces of character, or possessions that reflect a curious interest in the world. Replicating a showroom in your home may look nice, but it doesn't reveal much about who you are. Wabi-sabi celebrates objects with mysterious, unknown origins—handmade things, found pieces, items without brand names or status attached. Even if your design sense is more clean and modern, it's possible to incorporate special treasures that spark real happiness in you without also compromising your personal taste.

So what *are* the particulars? They're those belongings that remind you of what you're grateful for. While wabi-sabi is about paring away the unnecessary, this aesthetic and way of life is never minimal to the point of being cold or sterile. Rather, wabi-sabi is warm and inviting, compelling to the eye and to the spirit. In my home, almost every item I own reminds me of a story, a place, or an important relationship. It's Polaroids of loved ones by my bedside, dog-eared books on the coffee table, rocks from special trips and beach walks, framed letters from friends, and quotations taped to the fridge. It's treasured gifts from afar, old journals, and reupholstered garage-sale finds. These seemingly mundane details become important landmarks to anyone who walks through my door, pointing to where I find value and inspiration. These visual prompts help keep me true to who I am and who I want to be. As Winston Churchill once said, "We shape our dwellings, and then our dwellings shape us."

Let Forts Be Fun Again

—

Forts—or "child caves," as I like to refer to them—are those small, secluded spaces that kids seek out: under tables, within bushes, behind couches, inside cupboards, and below stairways. The phrase *child caves* comes from one of my favorite books, *A Pattern Language*, in which the authors talk about how important it is for children to have hideaways that are just their size, or at least small enough to fit only a friend or two. Thinking of these little spaces reminds us that as young people, we were drawn to places that safely enveloped us and—even better—were hidden from the adult world, where expectations abound. I'm not sure we ever stop needing shared secret places; we just grow up and tend to think we've outgrown "childish" tendencies as well. As a result, I think we miss out on some of the more magical places and moments that children naturally know how to enjoy.

My childhood was filled with tucked-away spaces like attics, closets, basements, hedges, forest hideaways, and treetops. The times I shared there with friends bonded me to them in ways I never experienced merely on the open playground. Many years later as an adult, I was lucky enough to have access to a very small second-floor outdoor porch. It overlooked downtown city buildings, and had a locking door for privacy and a Hawthorne tree beside it for shade. This place became known as the Nook, and it was a true refuge. Countless evenings were shared with friends in that little shelter, and many relationships were forged through conversations that may not have happened in any other setting. My childlike urge to enjoy tiny retreats with close companions has simply never gone away.

One way to reclaim this more lighthearted approach to connecting is to take cues from kids (and your childhood self). Watch the way they gravitate toward light-speckled, shadowy spaces under trees, and find comfort in nooks and crannies that are just their size. They've got the right idea when it comes to finding wabi-sabi settings that make us vulnerable with others, no matter our age. Environments that force us to touch knees, rub arms, or share leg space can't help but make us feel like spilling secrets as well. There are exceptions, of course (mainly public spaces like airplanes, buses, the subway; i.e., places where we have no choice but to be close), but when we sneak off to these "forts" on purpose, the physical closeness has a special effect on us.

This is not to persuade you to go find hidey-holes in the back bushes in which to throw parties (though if that idea appeals to you, by all means make it your secret garden to share). Rather, the point is to recognize that we really haven't changed so much. We still love hiding away in places that shelter and hug us in just the right ways—and these hideouts let us have the heart-to-hearts we often need. Maybe it's a broken-in love seat, a shady bench in your nearby park, a mini backyard patio, or simply a secluded corner of the house. No matter what kind of child cave you discover, the point is that sharing hidden places can deepen our relationships—and make for some pretty extraordinary memories.

The Intimate Table
Forget the Table

—

One of the best ways to spark an intimate occasion is to leave the table behind altogether. Some of my favorite memories are moments when we've forsaken the usual dining etiquette. Sometimes this happens by necessity and sometimes by choice. In our first home together, my husband and I ate every meal on the floor, on the bed, or off our laps on the porch cot simply because there wasn't enough space for a table. While this was inconvenient at times, I wouldn't trade these experiences for anything. Meals shared in unexciting places can still seem very special, even when they're far from fancy. A plain baguette, a wedge of cheese, a handful of fruit, a bar of chocolate, and a bottle of something sparkling make any occasion feel like a feast, no elegant china or flatware needed.

Being outdoors is especially wonderful because it puts you a little closer to your natural, wild side, giving you the opportunity to lie on your back in the sun, or kick off your shoes and let down your hair in a way you probably wouldn't when having company indoors. Suddenly we feel free to interact in familiar, casual ways we wouldn't at the dining table. We flick ants off each other. We sit on the grass and use each other's bodies as pillows. We graze on snacks and nap and forget propriety altogether.

The normal social anxieties that often keep us from getting comfortable with one another somehow decrease when we're in the backyard; at the park, lake, beach, or river; or in the woods. These occasions let us abandon the rules and embrace a simpler version of life where formalities like the table matter less, or not at all. Letting go of our idea of what hosting ought to look like opens us up to a world of possibilities—a wabi-sabi world that celebrates this more unorthodox way of living. Doing so means we are free to entertain wherever, and in whatever ways make us feel closest to those around us.

Eat with Your Hands

—

Year-round warm temperatures in California provide plenty of chances for laid-back eating, whether that means enjoying hot dogs at the beach, tacos in the backyard, or chips and guacamole at the park. These are the moments when I find myself forgetting about my phone, my to-do list, and the normal daily stresses. Eating with your hands instantly creates an easygoing atmosphere. This doesn't mean dinner can't still be elegant and beautiful—it just lets your guests get their hands dirty and gobble with gumption. Picture the difference between serving crab or lobster from the shell, where everyone picks and pries with their fingers, dipping morsels into melted butter, and dining on lobster tail that's been perfectly plated and can be easily eaten using a knife and fork. Both forms of enjoyment have their time and place, but the first way allows for us to *really* experience our food. More important, it changes how we interact with the people around us. Eating with our hands is a chance to literally break bread with our friends. The key is remembering how simple and healing this act can be.

Gather During the Golden Hours:
Post-Sunrise and Pre-Sunset

—

For as long as I can remember, every time my family has gone on a walk, a hike, or a drive or has simply eaten dinner in the backyard, my mother has always said, "Look at the light!" It wasn't until my high school years that I realized she was onto something. There's nothing quite like the morning and evening hours, when the sun casts a golden glow and shadows are long and blue—there's a reason why people call this the "magic hour." Everything has a warm radiance, and moments shared seem heightened. Part of what's so thrilling when the sun is low and the light nuanced is that these times are so fleeting. Nothing could be more wabi-sabi than this recognition that each day is extraordinary exactly because it's over so quickly.

Even though these golden moments usually occur when we're either busy getting ready for the day or exhausted from work and eager to slump on the couch, it's always worth investing in them. This kind of light can't come from lamps or even candles. Plus, it's important for our bodies to experience these periods of warmth in order to wake us up, and then also to prepare us for sundown. Sharing these brief times together can make an occasion out of something otherwise rather humdrum. Drinking coffee at sunrise with a friend or two or three can turn a normal ritual into a much-needed chance to feel understood at the start of the day. Gathering for snacks or a glass of wine on the porch near sunset allows us to share the events of the day. A wabi-sabi welcome is not about the elaborate party or the grand gesture—instead it's about taking advantage of these easily missed opportunities to experience beauty together, simple as they may be.

CALIFORNIA

Find a Good Picnic Basket

—

Picnics are a great training ground for loosening up. Though this book is about encouraging you to host at home, it's essential to take advantage of the outdoors when the weather is good—just because you've ditched the house doesn't mean you can't still play host. Investing in a durable basket means you'll always be ready to dash outside with snacks and blanket in tow, even on a last-minute whim. In my experience, everyone appreciates it when someone else initiates adventures of this kind, especially if the instigator is willing to bring the food and other necessities. All the rules of wabi-sabi-inspired hosting still apply—you're just moving beyond the walls of your house. Some of my favorite meals have been picnics, largely because they've not only been shared in good company but generally also have taken place in an exceptional setting.

A few of the most important things to pack are a sharp knife; a cutting surface of some sort (I usually bring along a small wooden cutting board); cloth napkins or dish towels (which helps to avoid generating trash); a few forks; metal plates; a bottle of water; small glasses (if I'm really prepared); a little container of salt; and, of course, the food. My standard picnic fare usually consists of cheese, salami, crackers or bread, some fruit, a cucumber (or another easily consumed veggie), trail mix, and chocolate. If I'm feeling ambitious, maybe I'll bring along a salad or a dish I've prepared at home. Other times when I just can't bring myself to make much of an effort, I'll pick up a pizza, sandwiches, or sushi along the way. All of these items are easily eaten with your hands. The simpler the food, the less difficult it is to get out the door, and the less cleanup afterward.

Whatever the spread, a picnic blanket creates the quintessential intimate space. Maybe I like picnics so much because by nature, they create cozy, perfectly imperfect scenarios. I can't be too uptight about much, because try as I might, there is nothing I can do about ever-present bugs, spilled drinks, and blackberry stains on the blanket—and sometimes the most unexpected additions to our plans make the occasion even more wonderful.

PRACTICAL
MATTERS

Ask thoughtful questions and don't be afraid to candidly answer the same ones. Try to be open and honest about what's going on in your life, even if it feels awkward or embarrassing at first.

—

Invite friends and family into the kitchen and don't be shy about asking for help. Delegate! Many people appreciate being given a task.

—

Greet guests with a hug, a hand on the shoulder, or a warm handshake. Don't be afraid to extend a friendly touch.

—

When you're feeling overwhelmed, take a short time-out and inhale slowly for a few deep breaths. Go to your room and do some jumping jacks to work off excess energy. It's important to care about the details, but don't get so worked up about perfection that you miss out on enjoying the occasion.

—

Create a serene home by taking tips from nature—pick calming colors, leave empty spaces, and include found objects from the outdoors that delight you.

—

Be generous and open with your home. Invite friends to drop by unannounced—they should be able to show up without a call or a text and still be welcomed graciously.

—

Create a home that's true to who you are, reflects your values, and inspires you all at the same time. Display meaningful items like love notes, quotations, children's art (or your own), and old photographs in obvious places, like the bathroom, the fridge, or framed on the wall.

—

Embrace your childlike spirit by hanging out in makeshift tents or cabanas in the backyard, hammocks, hidden nooks, small, shadowy spaces, and so on. Invite friends to enjoy these spaces, too.

—

Seek out untraditional places to host guests, whether a hidden nook in your yard, a nearby park, or somewhere farther afield. Ditch the table for something a little more exciting and memorable.

—

Choose settings to eat together where you can sit close and be cozy with one another, like benches, picnic blankets, a bistro table, or a small breakfast nook.

—

Gather when the sun is low in the sky and the light is diffused, like early in the morning or right before sunset.

—

Become someone who picnics! And buy yourself a good picnic basket that's always stocked with the essentials so you can dash out of the house on short notice when the weather's fine.

OPPOSITE

This incredibly delicious raw, vegan "cheesecake" was made by a thirteen-year-old (Wanda Weller's son, Arley)—a testament to the fact that we can all be cooks and bakers with a little practice and effort!

SETTING THE TABLE

Backyard, beach, or grassy-patch get-togethers are all about no-fuss meals and table settings. Instead, the beauty of these gatherings comes from the haphazard way all your food and drink options fill the table or picnic blanket. No need for anything fancy when you're surrounded by the outdoors! Throw in some napkins and you're ready to go. Here's a sampling of some of my favorite items that make for an easy, minimal-prep gathering that's lovely to look at, too.

— Hearty crackers or a fresh baguette that's easily torn by hand
— One or two wedges/rounds of soft cheese
— Earthy, seed-filled jam like fig or raspberry
— A bowl of plain, soft dates (I like Medjool best for snacking) or dates stuffed with almonds
— Dried apricots
— Sliced or peeled oranges or grapefruit
— Strawberries, raspberries, or blueberries
— Sliced salami or prosciutto
— Marcona almonds
— Grapes
— Sliced, salted cucumbers
— Lemon water, sparkling water, iced tea, or wine

Stone Fruit with Honey-Vanilla Goat Cheese

These treats are perfect for simple evening dinners and potlucks in the backyard. Any stone fruit (like peaches, nectarines, plums, or even cherries) will do, but apricots are an especially good size for easy snacking. The version pictured was made with yellow peaches. I used to live close to a creamery that made honey-vanilla goat cheese, but now I make my own; it's ridiculously delicious.

Halve or quarter the fruit and remove the pits.

Whip together softened plain goat cheese, a bit of local honey, and a few drops of good-quality vanilla extract and put a dollop of this into each piece of hollowed-out fruit. If you don't like goat cheese, any cheese with a similar texture will do.

Once the fruit is plated, I like to drizzle maple syrup or (more!) honey over it and sprinkle a handful of crushed nuts like walnuts, pecans, or whatever I have in the cupboard on top. The sticky syrup or honey helps the crushed nuts stay on top. Keep in the fridge until ready to serve, then enjoy!

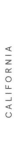

All-Season Tacos

Tacos are a true staple of the California diet—mostly because they're so quick, delicious, and easy to tailor to personal taste. They are the perfect meal for a warm summer evening on the deck, but they can also make an incredibly satisfying dish for brisker weather if you bulk up the ingredients a bit. Here are just a few different ways you can approach tacos, depending on your taste buds.

First, start with your tortillas: wheat or corn. Naturally, you can find these at the grocery store or at a local Mexican market (which we have in abundance in California but which may not be prominent elsewhere); or, if you're feeling really adventurous, you can make your own. I tried this recently and it's harder than it looks, but the important thing is to have (or borrow) a tortilla press and wax or parchment paper. Then buy some masa harina and follow the instructions on the package or look up a recipe. Most recipes call for nothing more than cornmeal, water, and some salt—perhaps a touch of lime.

Next, gather your staples. I like to have lime wedges, chopped cilantro, salsa, and *cotija* (a white, slightly soft but crumbly Mexican cheese) on hand for any variety of taco. These are the elements you should have no matter what you're putting into your tacos.

For veggie tacos, some go-tos include chopped tomatoes, sliced avocado or guacamole, diced red or white onion, fresh corn, slivered radish, sautéed peppers, and black or pinto beans. (You can use beans from a can, or soak dry beans overnight and then boil them.)

Continued

Another simple combo I like for tacos is sweet potato and black beans. Chop the sweet potatoes (about one large sweet potato per two people) into ½-inch cubes and toss with olive oil, salt, and a swirl of maple syrup before spreading onto a baking tray (line it with a sheet of parchment paper—otherwise the syrup will caramelize and burn on your pan). Bake at 375°F for about 20 minutes, or until slightly brown on the edges but still soft inside. Simmer the black beans on the stove over low heat, seasoning with a bit of salt and cumin.

If you want meat in the mix, I like using chicken from a leftover roast or an already cooked breast that can be shredded, but any meat, fish, or seafood will do. To season, put the shredded chicken into a skillet with enough salsa of your choosing to cover the meat entirely. Cook slowly over low heat for 10 to 15 minutes, adding small amounts of water as necessary to keep the chicken moist and tender, stirring occasionally. Sprinkle in a bit of salt and pepper as desired. .

Pile your chosen ingredients onto the tortilla any which way, squeeze on a bit of lime and some cilantro, top with *cotija*, and enjoy!

Mint and Lemon Salad

Mint and lemon are staples in my diet; I use them in salads, in my water glass, in smoothies, on veggies, in pasta—both are incredibly versatile and super refreshing.

Start with a base layer of greens of your choosing, like shredded or baby kale, spinach leaves, or arugula. If you're using mature kale, make sure to massage the leaves with a bit of olive oil, lemon juice, and salt to help tenderize them and cut the bitterness. A small handful of greens per person is usually sufficient if it's a side salad—obviously you'll need more if the salad is the entrée.

Pluck two or three leaves of fresh mint per person, and tear each leaf into several pieces before combining them with the greens. Feel free to add more mint if you desire.

Depending on the season, I like mixing in different ingredients that complement the mint. Diced beets are delicious in the cooler seasons (I prepare them by boiling and peeling the skin off once soft). Thinly sliced radishes are lovely in spring, but for summer, a combination of fresh corn and halved cherry or grape tomatoes is a must. For something even sweeter, try sliced or chopped peaches or nectarines. Whatever you choose, keep it simple; use just one fruit or veggie (along with the greens and mint).

For a light dressing, I like to whisk together some olive oil, lemon juice, salt, and honey or maple syrup. If I'm feeling slightly more ambitious, I'll add mustard, chopped garlic, or very thinly sliced shallots or red onions (or all three!) to this mixture—I may even throw in a few more torn mint leaves. I rarely measure this combination (preferring to add to taste), but here is a basic ratio for reference:

- 3 to 4 tablespoons olive oil
  (start with 3 and add more as necessary)
- 2 tablespoons lemon juice
- 1 teaspoon honey or maple syrup
- ½ teaspoon Dijon mustard (optional)
- ½ teaspoon chopped garlic
- 10 thin slices shallot or onion
- Pinch of salt

This makes about ⅓ cup of dressing, which should be enough for a few small salads. Leftover dressing can be kept in the refrigerator for up to 3 days if stored in an airtight container.

To top it all off, crumble a soft cheese like goat or feta over the greens, or use a shredded hard cheese, like Parmesan or pecorino. Finish the salad with a final sprinkle of sea salt, such as Maldon, and a grind or two of black pepper.

France

Chapter Four

EARTHY AND ALIVE

Look to the Wild, Unrefined
World for Inspiration

Southern France is wild, rustic, and wonderfully alive. Hilltop towns, fields of red poppies, old farmhouses, and wavy cypress trees fill its panoramas, and white horses roam freely along its salty coast. Sometimes it seems that nature has complete reign here, finding its way through the cracks of every cobblestone street. Except for the palatial buildings and fancily pruned gardens left behind by past kings, unkempt ruggedness pervades even the most well-cared-for places. My impression is that everyday life for the French is closely connected to the earth—they fully embrace a little roughness around the edges, and somehow seem all the more elegant for it. I particularly admire their knack for accepting nature's unrefined beauty instead of trying to restrain or subdue it.

I see this in treasured buildings left weather-beaten from top to bottom, and in the untamed, deserted dunes along the coast where little else but lighthouses dot the shores. Just like the wabi-sabi way of life, the French perspective delights in these so-called imperfections and wild spaces. This easy acceptance of nature likely comes from the fact that in many places, village walls give way to vast openness rather than suburban sprawl or strip malls. I've often hiked straight into the mountains from the edge of town, or wandered into wild fields and olive groves not far from the *centre ville*. These villages are themselves rough around the edges, and this phenomenon seems to inspire every part of life here.

I consider the treasured times I've spent in the south of France as some of my most alive, alert, and aware; something about being there revitalizes the senses, making me more conscious of all that the natural world has to offer. I can recall the rich taste of a mushroom soufflé, the smell of dried lavender, and the sound of plane trees rustling in the wind just as easily as I can feel the hot July sun on my skin, see mounds of soft apricots and peaches at the market, and hear the summer *cigales* (cicadas) chattering outside my window. Life in France is rich with flavor, fragrance, and a contentment I've experienced in few other places, and I've found here that a ready welcome of the elements and the unexpected, flaws and all, brings unmatched inspiration and invigoration. The following are some of the principles I see guiding life in France—healthy reminders of how to weave what's unpolished and unplanned into our daily experiences, and how to be happy about it. I have taken them to heart, and perhaps you'll find them useful, too.

*Chantal Dussouchaud has an enviably buoyant
disposition that truly embodies the c'est la vie attitude.
Here, in her home in Le Cannet, where she lives with her
husband, Harry, and daughter, Sophie, she takes things as
they come and lets things roll off her back—a habit that
comes in especially handy when she's working on her various
interior design projects, which inevitably have setbacks.*

The Earthy Host

Learn to Say C'est la Vie

—

This familiar French saying breezily captures the wabi-sabi sensibility of accepting whatever comes. *C'est la vie* means "That's life," or "Such is life," and is usually something we say when circumstances are less than ideal; learning to react this way can help us be more gracious, even when we're not feeling especially forgiving. Life in France, especially in smaller towns, requires being agreeable and easygoing because things are predictably unreliable—shops and markets are likely to be closed just as you discover you need something, bus lines are on strike when you want to venture to a nearby city, and restaurants are shut down for the afternoon precisely when you want a bite to eat. In some sense, the French have come to expect the unexpected, but instead of getting worked up over minor inconveniences, they shrug them off with characteristic nonchalance.

During even the relatively short stints I've spent in France, I've learned to let go of my typical American agenda and to allow a c'est la vie approach guide me. Some of my favorite memories stem from setting out with few expectations

and letting myself be surprised, like the times I've gotten lost down alleyways and stumbled upon an old bookstore or a hidden *boulangerie*. Back at home, it's not always easy to have such a laid-back attitude, but this kind of relaxed perspective can aid us anywhere, especially when we're entertaining.

As mentioned in the California chapter, things that are annoying, frustrating, or likely to fluster you are going to happen when you're hosting, and it's up to you to decide how to react. Countless times, I've had all of my grand hopes fall apart in the midst of planning—only to discover that the alternative, spontaneous result is better than anything I could have come up with myself. Rain comes unexpectedly so we rig up a makeshift but dreamy bohemian-looking shelter; or the chocolate soufflé falls so we eat vanilla ice cream topped with the deliciously gooey, fudgy remains. Instead of clinging to how you envisioned things would unfold, try a c'est la vie outlook and you may just be rewarded for your flexibility. As my husband and I regularly say, "Not as expected, but better than imagined."

An earthy, organic sense of beauty can be seen everywhere at Camellas-Lloret, the maison d'hôtes *run by Annie Moore and her husband, Colin, in a small village called Montréal. With a laid-back but attentive approach to hospitality, Annie has imbued every corner of this place with a keen sense of what raw elegance looks, tastes, and feels like.*

Adopt a More Natural Approach . . . to Everything

—

Learning to appreciate a more organic sense of beauty can change the way we see everything around us, including ourselves. Everything in France seems to exude an unrefined elegance, and French women in particular are known for a seemingly effortless but enviably graceful air. What accounts for this casual charm? I think it comes from accepting and celebrating how things naturally look, taste, and feel instead of opting for something more refined or processed; this is true whether we're selecting oddly shaped produce from the market or letting our hair go silver. One way to encourage this kind of attitude is by applying a pure, unpolished philosophy to just about everything: the way we cook, enjoy food, dress ourselves, decorate our homes, and approach aging, and, of course, how we host.

Embracing what's unpolished doesn't require becoming a full-blown hippie, but it does mean taking the time to slow down and enjoy the mundane tasks of everyday life like cooking and self-care as great pleasures instead of challenges or nuisances—and, of course, choosing to celebrate what's unique and natural to you. Indulging in such pleasures might involve taking greater care of your skin so you can wear less makeup (or go without it entirely); cooking with real butter or ghee (clarified butter) rather than a less flavorful stand-in; having a simple but sophisticated "uniform" you regularly wear; or gathering with friends in a muddy garden instead of an upscale restaurant—leave the high heels and nice clothes at home! A more open-ended, diverse sense of what brings us joy and is beautiful makes the world a more compelling place because we're able to appreciate wonderfully disparate things—whether it be a nose covered with freckles or a home full of wabi-sabi character.

Embrace le Joie de Vivre *and* l'Art de Vivre

—

A healthy sense of wonder allows us to experience more joy and artfulness in the everyday, enlivening every aspect of life, including how we entertain. I first experienced the magic of a warm croissant and milky hot chocolate for breakfast as a ten-year-old in Paris; this minor indulgence convinced me that the people of France know a thing or two about enjoying themselves. The French could teach us quite a lot about *le joie* and *l'art de vivre*, since much of life there seems to revolve around the appreciation and awe of simple pleasures. What else can explain *crêpes* and *macarons* being sold on every street corner, town squares consistently filled with café-goers, and river quays lined with lovers embracing? These subtle joys at the center of society reveal a life philosophy of delight, prompting us to savor each day with a lighthearted, spontaneous spirit.

This way of being proclaims that artful living comes through paying better attention; there are marvels everywhere if only we have eyes to see them. Countless celebrated artists—Toulouse-Lautrec, Van Gogh, Monet, Manet, Cézanne, Picasso, Renoir, Degas, Seurat—have captured these wonders through their paintings of daily life in France, demonstrating that the real essence of life can be found in the most modest, understated moments, especially when we're spending time together. I can't help but think of how content, relaxed, and alive the old men playing *boules* in the village parks always seem to be; they appear to understand that life's true pleasures can be found in relishing occasions like these.

How do we start experiencing this zest for life, especially if and when our days feel rather ordinary? A wabi-sabi approach starts with simply observing everything around us more closely and appreciating things that usually go unnoticed: the scent of jasmine from the neighbor's yard; a perfectly (or imperfectly) poached egg; filtered sunlight dancing on the wall. Or maybe it's investing in an activity that starts your day with admiration: a brisk walk or hike, an ocean swim, reading on the patio, listening to music, journaling or writing a letter. Wabi-sabi things and instances are sometimes said to inspire a "sad-beautiful" feeling, which sounds a little melancholy, but I don't think it's all that far off from experiencing the brighter sense of joie de vivre. Both sensations simply remind us that each moment is worth basking in because it won't be with us forever.

The Earthy Home

Showcase the Wrinkled Linens

—

Perhaps what I love most about a French sensibility is that it's incredibly relaxed, finding loveliness in nonuniform, naturally imperfect items and places. Nearly everything in France feels unique: there's an irregular quality to homes, cobblestone streets, overgrown foliage, mismatched window shutters, and the unparallel plane trees that line the streets. Structures aren't "perfect," but instead are freeform and adapted to surrounding conditions; a stone wall veers off course to go around a tree or a door is hung off-kilter to accommodate a building tilted over time. To me, this variation symbolizes a feeling of aliveness, since really *alive* things are often a little wild, uncontained, and chaotic, like an untamed forest or ocean waves. Bringing liveliness into our homes means allowing parts of it to feel undomesticated and free.

Embracing this more easygoing aesthetic allows us to have a little more fun, whether that means using mismatched stoneware or glassware, setting the table with rumpled linen napkins, or decorating the house with big, unruly bunches of wildflowers and weeds. Choosing a down-to-earth approach when we entertain gives us more freedom, but it also liberates our guests, since people usually feel most at ease in a carefree environment. If this approach comes very unnaturally to you, start small and pick one thing to focus on in an unorthodox way. That might mean cooking a more low-key meal than you normally would or making a table centerpiece from Queen Anne's lace instead of your tried-and-true tulips. If you tend to worry about others' expectations (like I do), all you need to say by way of explanation for your unironed tablecloth is that it's the "French way"—and who can argue with that?

Decorate with Nature

—

Just as you can use nature to create calm, decorating with it can be the simplest way to make your home feel more alive. In France, these qualities are often built right into people's houses: Walls are constructed with rugged rock, and ceilings are lined with rough, exposed wooden beams. But even if you don't have a naturally rustic home, there are other straightforward ways to bring life into your space by incorporating wilder elements.

Start by investing in real plants. Introducing living, breathing greenery into our homes can be a major improvement that doesn't require a lot of money or time. There's no need to produce an all-out jungle, but putting a live plant in each main room of the house is a good beginning. If you have a hopelessly black thumb and plants tend to be a waste of money, look instead for oversized leaves, fronds, or branches you can occasionally buy to freshen up your space—a monstera, a palm, or a blooming plum can work particularly well. Even if it's temporary, any bit of green has a way of reviving our homes and our spirits.

You can also introduce nature into your home by using unexpected objects for practical needs, like a round rock as a doorstop, or a straight branch to hang curtains or hand towels from. A rough-edged wood plank can be used for shelving along the wall or suspended across the tub for soaps and sponges. Large, smooth sticks like driftwood or birch branches can be bunched in the corner or in sturdy pots to add character to a room, and small stumps can be used as side tables. On a smaller scale, dried bits of trees and plants—think lavender or pink peppercorns—can add a touch of subtle color to a coffee table or the mantel, whether in a bowl or a vase or displayed loosely by themselves. One of my favorite things about decorating this way (other than that it's free) is that there's no waste involved—once you grow tired of something, you can return it to the backyard, put it in the compost, or add it to the fire. Bringing these unrefined elements into our homes helps link us, and our guests, to the wider world beyond our walls, reminding and inspiring us to get out of doors as often as possible.

Let the Breeze Blow Through

—

I've always felt most comfortable in spaces where doors and windows are left open (weather permitting): As most of us can attest, air and sunlight completely change the way any room looks and feels—and the way we feel inside it. The French realized this early on (during the seventeenth century, in fact), which led them to invent what are now known as "French doors": glass-lined doors that usually lead out to a terrace or balcony. Letting nature freely permeate our homes can affect us in many important ways: It lifts our mood, makes our spaces feel more open, heals us faster (both physically and mentally, as many studies have proven), and generally improves our all-around well-being. Even in urban settings where "nature" may not be close by, keeping windows and shades open lets us hear birds, feel the breeze, and watch clouds move across the sky.

A wabi-sabi aesthetic is big on filtered light, so if you have too much harsh light, hang thin, gauzy curtains inside or a slatted bamboo curtain outside. Or if your space is low on light, use some well-placed mirrors to help capture and reflect whatever natural rays you *do* get. Likewise, if you're not regularly able to keep windows and doors open, a fan can do wonders for circulating any bit of fresh air. Elementary as the idea may seem, living things need light and oxygen not only to survive but to thrive. I always feel happier when I'm outside, but if household chores or cooking dinner keeps me indoors, I have a habit of opening the house as much as possible, and I usually keep everything ajar long after dark.

I also love bringing the indoors out as much as I like bringing the outdoors in. I tend to transform any outdoor space I have into a living area, complete with lounge chairs, pillows, tables, potted plants, and lights. The more I'm able to minimize the divide between these two spaces, the more seamlessly I move between them throughout the day.

The Earthy Table

Have a Table That Tells Stories

—

Mealtimes are sacred in France, which makes the table a very special fixture in any French household. Because it's often the center of activity, it takes on a personal and practical nature: It's a place for multitasking, relaxing, eating good food, and enjoying conversation. It's a hardworking piece of furniture whether we gather around it for most meals (like the French) or not. Given all the use they get, our tables take on imperfections over time, and that's perfectly okay. The stories that accumulate through the permanent marks are what make us grow attached to and sentimental about the object itself—even if some scars came from a previous owner. My own table has wine rings, water spots, dried glue from art projects, and knife gouges from a dinner guest who apparently thought it was also a cutting board. After the initial mild annoyance over these "flaws," I always end up accepting that the table is meant to be functional, and therefore, additions like these aren't worth bothering over.

This easygoing philosophy can extend to the rest of our furniture, too. One end of a well-loved bench in my home is stained darker than the other, thanks to the time I placed a hard stick of butter in a patch of sun there to soften it for making cookies. Before I noticed it was long past soft, it had melted all over the legs. Not only did the mishap expose the walnut wood grain more fully, it also made for a humorous story that exposes my own scatterbrained nature. Likewise, the belongings that mean the most to me are the ones with stories attached, even if the objects aren't perfect in the traditional sense. I love the strangely proportioned furniture I made while in graduate school, roughed-up blankets and rugs found during travels or at flea markets, and quirky objects acquired from friends and family. The scratches, dents, and cracks that our possessions acquire over time are precisely what make our homes intimate and interesting, improving our spaces rather than spoiling them. Whatever your own tales may be, filling your home with objects that have meaning is ultimately what makes it a place worth loving and sharing with others.

Use Fresh Ingredients That
Show Their Flaws

—

It's nearly impossible to think of France without also thinking of French food, and at the heart of what makes this cuisine so delectable is the caliber and freshness of its ingredients. You'd be hard-pressed to find many towns or villages throughout France that don't have a regular farmers' market, which provides access to good-quality, locally grown food. By "quality" I mean responsibly grown, small-yield goods that have been very recently picked and show some flaws—muddy turnips; carrots with warty growths; and vibrant, oversized leafy greens. Produce that comes in varied colors and sizes with minor nicks or bruises is likely to be the least tampered with in terms of chemicals or genetic modification; if bugs are interested in your produce, it probably means it's worth eating. If you don't have a farmers' market nearby, use any available sources to find really fresh and untreated ingredients; this might be a nearby farm stand, a backyard garden, a corner store, or your neighbor's pear tree. The point is to take advantage of whatever is readily accessible to you rather than rely solely on items that have been grown on huge corporate farms and then shipped halfway around the world. And, tastes aside, a lopsided, bulbous heirloom tomato will always be more beautiful in wabi-sabi terms than a conventional, perfectly oval hothouse Roma.

OPPOSITE

*Introduced to me as simply "Granny," this amazing
mother of thirteen, now in her nineties, still makes
daily feasts for a rotating cast of visiting children,
grandchildren, and neighbors.*

FOLLOWING PAGES

*Annie adds cilantro to a giant pan (borrowed from her
local butcher) of paella—a dish inspired by nearby
Spain—for a large dinner gathering of friends from
both near and far. For dessert, she serves a perfectly
rustic apricot tart.*

Explore Earthy Textures and Tastes

—

In France, eating is considered one of life's most luxurious pleasures—which is saying a lot, given how much pleasure the French find in most things. French dining is full of rich textures and tastes, and there's no holding back: thick cream, whipped eggs, butter, chocolate, strong cheese, full-bodied wine, fluffy pastry dough, nuts, savory herbs, hearty meats . . . there's a reason that French food is synonymous with satisfaction. Cooking like this—with pure, simple ingredients—is all about uncovering and drawing out as much flavor as possible rather than dwelling on calories, carbs, or cholesterol. As Julia Child and her colleagues tell us in the introduction to *Mastering the Art of French Cooking*, "All of the techniques employed in French cooking are aimed at one goal: How does it taste?"

Enjoying our food and the process of making it should be the priority when we cook, especially when it comes to hosting others. I only have to think of the French word *gourmand* to be reminded of this mind-set, though I prefer to think of this in terms of being a happy eater rather than a finicky connoisseur with an upturned nose. A gourmand is excited by all varieties of textures and tastes without being overly concerned with a long list of dietary restrictions or rules. Choosing this attitude toward food can be wonderfully liberating, and, I would argue, a completely healthful way to enjoy eating together—especially in a culture obsessed with food fads and endless substitutions, and, frankly, in which too much guilt is associated with eating. As the French well know, food can be a beautiful and celebratory part of life, and though every good celebration requires moderation, a shared sense of conviviality can make us all feel more alive.

PRACTICAL MATTERS

Exercising a c'est la vie approach means going with the flow and letting things unfold spontaneously—or quickly coming up with a fitting alternative when need be. Maybe this means creatively changing the dinner menu when the store's out of salmon, or making do when you accidentally over-roast the chicken.

—

Freshen up your mundane routines by taking a more natural approach. Instead of using bleached white eggs from the grocery store, try sourcing earthy (i.e., they still have remnants from the coop) brown, blue, or light green eggs from a local farm or market. Rather than blow-dry your hair over the weekend, head out the door with a wild, curly mane. Sift through your closet and pare it down to just a few things that make you feel great.

—

Make a list of some of the ways you find the joy and beauty in the everyday; this might simply be things you feel grateful for, or moments that make you laugh, cry, smile, or pause on a regular basis. If you're having a hard time thinking of things that make you truly curious, excited, or filled with awe, maybe it's time to slow down and reacquaint yourself with some simple pleasures you can enjoy daily.

—

Forget the steam iron and feel free to pull out the wrinkled linens when guests are over. Natural fibers often look best in a perfectly rumpled state—just like wildflowers look best when you let them be a little wild. If real linen's not an option, use cloth flour sacks, which have a similar earthy look and effect.

—

Every kind of home can benefit from touches of nature, whether it's a suburban tract house or a rustic cabin in the woods. Use objects from nature for practical purposes, like a rough rock by the door for scraping off mud, or just to appreciate, like leafy plants or a stack of smooth stones on the piano.

—

Open up your home to the outdoors as much as possible—and bring the indoors out as well. Prop open doors, windows, shades, drapes, or blinds, and get fresh air flowing. Similarly, make living spaces outside with lounge chairs, cots, pillows, a hammock, and small or large dining spaces so that you can move seamlessly between indoors and out.

—

Invest in furniture that's built to endure and can acquire marks and stories over time. Some of the most solid and inspiring pieces can be found used or secondhand; look in thrift stores and at garage sales or flea markets for well-made items that can acquire new meaning and memories in your own home.

—

Whenever you can, eat and cook with fresh produce that has bruises and bumps, in a range of colors. Fill the fridge and counter with flawed and fragrant ingredients; the more unprocessed and unpackaged, the better.

—

Let texture and taste be your guide when it comes to cooking. Indulge in the "real stuff" like butter, heavy cream, and fragrant cheese (at least some of the time) instead of flavorless substitutions—just compensate by learning to eat French-size (i.e., smaller) portions.

SETTING THE TABLE

Emulating the French in the kitchen can be the gateway to a more relaxed, livelier approach to eating—if not all the time, at least on weekends or when you're entertaining. Baguette! Butter! Cheese! Wine! All those things we typically feel we shouldn't indulge in can be enjoyed and savored in full. If French cooking seems a bit intimidating, just start simply and work your way up from there. Invest in Julia Child's compendium or look at blogs for ideas about where to begin. The nice thing about French fare is that usually the objective isn't to make exotic or unusual food (not unusual to a French mind, at least), but rather to take very standard dishes and make them taste exceptionally good.

For instance, you might compose a salad of fresh, flavorful greens with a shallot-heavy vinaigrette; roast some herbed veggies like carrots and asparagus; toast some buttery, garlicky bread; roast a meat or sausage you especially like; and top it off with a flourless chocolate cake or a thick chocolate pudding. And, naturally, if you really want to feel French, finish the evening with a cheese plate. Comté, Camembert, and Roquefort are all stalwarts, but don't be afraid to try something a little out of the box. I'm no wine expert, but you can ask someone at your wine store to make a recommendation based on what you're serving. This might not be the feast you set out to try on any given Tuesday, but it's the right kind of meal for a Saturday or Sunday when you have most of the day to putter around the kitchen, whipping up something new. Toss together a wild, grassy bouquet and pull out your wrinkly linens and your mother's old silverware, and your table's ready to go. The most important part is to give yourself enough time to really revel in what you've created and, of course, to share it with others!

Fancy Toast

This is the perfect dish for treating friends to a long, leisurely Saturday brunch with several cups of coffee and orange juice.

Start with a loaf of hearty bread—I like multigrain or seeded varieties with a thick crust, but something like sourdough or classic French bread could work as well. Slice into thick pieces. Usually I make my slices too thick for the toaster, in which case toasting in the broiler works beautifully.

While your bread is toasting, poach an egg (or eggs). There are many techniques for doing this, but I rely on Julia Child's approach in *Mastering the Art of French Cooking*. Once the bread is toasted, slather it with a spreadable cheese of your choosing (such as goat cheese, ricotta, or cream cheese), and follow with a thick layer of raspberry jam. Top with the poached egg and a bit of salt. If I'm really feeling fancy, I'll layer on a few edible flowers, or some green sprouts for a slightly savory addition.

Pair with any fresh fruit.

Roasted Yams or
Sweet Potatoes with
Butter and Herbs

This makes for the easiest of side dishes, or dress it up for a more substantial entrée.

Preheat the oven to 400°F.

Rinse a yam (or sweet potato), pat dry, and rub with a bit of olive oil before setting it on a baking sheet or in a ceramic dish and roasting in the oven until soft, roughly 45 minutes.

Remove the yam from the oven, slice it lengthwise down the middle, and put a few pats of butter in the center, along with flaky salt, freshly ground black pepper, and chopped herbs like thyme, rosemary, or *herbes de Provence*. For just a touch of additional sweetness (though it likely won't need it), drizzle with maple syrup.

If you want to make this into a meal, sauté a couple of handfuls of greens with olive oil, garlic, and a bit of lemon juice. Then top the potato with the greens, a poached egg, and a sprinkle of salty cheese.

Oven-Roasted Chicken with Green Garlic, Shallots, Lemon, and Thyme

Roast chicken is always a satisfying anchor for a simple meal that doesn't require much prep time. A 3½- to 4-pound chicken will feed four.

Preheat the oven to 325°F.

Trim the stems off 4 to 6 green garlic bulbs (young garlic with stems still attached) and stuff them into the chicken cavity, along with a small bunch of fresh thyme sprigs. Tie the legs together with twine. Place the chicken in a baking or casserole dish and rub the whole body with butter, placing a few pats under the skin. Season with salt, pepper, and a bit of fresh lemon juice.

Roughly chop any remaining garlic stems from the bunch, halve the green garlic bulbs, and tuck around the dish, along with 1 whole chopped shallot, 3 to 5 peeled garlic cloves, lemon wedges, and fresh thyme sprigs. Drizzle olive oil over the top.

Roast, rotating the shallots, garlic, and lemons occasionally, until the chicken is browned and tender and the garlic is very soft, 2½ to 3 hours. Serve with whatever you fancy!

Chapter Five

AMUSE THE SENSES

Use Taste, Touch, Sound, Smell, and Sight
to Create Wholly Sensuous Experiences

Italy is an utter celebration of the senses, resplendent with over-the-top artistry and lavishness. But amid all the grandeur, ornamentation, and excess, Italians also find joy in simple pleasures, be it a shot of morning espresso, a family walk through ancient olive groves, or a casual rendezvous with friends, regardless of the hour. Italy presents a paradox, merging the high culture and opulence of the Vatican, da Vinci, and Prada with the everyday delights of zippy Vespas, jars of Nutella, and freshly washed laundry drying on the line. It's a place where you'll see suave *ragazzi* twirling girls in the piazza, old men impeccably dressed in linen suits, and middle-aged nuns savoring the improbable combination of red wine and Coca-Cola. Life here is enjoyed through all the senses, with expressive hand gestures, flavorful meals, and *r*'s trilled in wonderful words like *buongiorno*.

I had my first meaningful encounter with Italian culture as a twenty-year-old studying art and literature in the Umbrian town of Orvieto, and the experience exhilarated me from beginning to end. All spring long a whirring hum of bees surrounded the hilltop city, pigeons cooed from rafters, lilacs spread their fragrance, and nettles stung my ankles on afternoon walks as monks from the nearby monastery called *"Vieni qua!"* (Come here!) to their big white dog,

Lupo. Daily dishes of pasta and vegetables liberally topped with cheese became the norm, and weekly visits to the open-air market surprised me with produce like fava beans and brilliant green figs that I'd never seen before. Each new venture, mundane or marvelous, demanded my complete attention—I didn't want to miss a thing.

My time spent in this ultra-aware state taught me that when our senses are completely engaged, the present is heightened and something special occurs: The more we see, taste, hear, smell, and feel the world around us, the more *real*, *vibrant*, and *dynamic* life becomes—we discover just how beautiful living truly is. Wabi-sabi describes beauty as something that happens to us; it's an event that takes place between us and something else rather than just a pretty thing we admire. I think this "event" is what the Italians do so well, because their sensuous passion allows them to perceive and experience something extraordinary in otherwise ordinary things and moments. I've found the Italian way of life to be an exemplary teacher, as it models how to let beauty *happen* to us through our fingertips, taste buds, ears, eyes, and nose. Practicing hospitality allows us to create these sensorial moments of beauty for others—and for ourselves—and the following are just a few of the ways I've seen it done with lovely success.

FOLLOWING PAGES

This festive gathering of friends and extended family was a celebration dinner in honor of a newly completed roof on a very old, traditional Italian country home. We were hosted by the local shoemaker of Orvieto, Federico Badia, and his wife, Hannah. The greetings that kicked off this get-together involved hugs, kisses, bottles of prosecco popping, toasts, cries of Ecco lo! (meaning something like "behold!"), and dogs barking. Gusto indeed.

The Sensuous Host

Greet with Gusto

—

Italians are naturally expressive people; they gesture emphatically with their hands, talk vigorously, and aren't afraid to kiss newcomers upon arrival. A warm, open-armed welcome from an Italian is something to remember: to experience it is to see a host express visible passion for every guest who passes through the door, and to understand that hospitality is something that can be shared through words, body language, and spirit. In fact, *gusto* in Italian actually means "flavor" or "taste," and there's never any question when I've been greeted with *flavor* versus something a little more, well, bland. Being met with a bit of liveliness always reassures me that my presence is desired—whether I'm in someone's home, meeting friends at a restaurant, or at a casual backyard party.

There are many ways to show your guests that you're truly glad to see them—greet them by name (and occasionally use it throughout any conversation), welcome them with touch (as noted in the California chapter), make eye contact, and readily say how appreciative you are of their presence. These acts of recognition can take place whether you're hosting a party of one or thirty-five; every guest should feel entirely welcome.

You don't have to be naturally extroverted to express these sentiments, either; quieter hosts can practice gusto in a way that feels personal and natural, too. My own way of connecting with newly arrived guests and friends is more often through subtle visual and physical cues, like an expressive face and a gentle touch, rather than by bounding across the room to throw my arms around someone. You can also receive your guests exuberantly by meeting them at the door with a cold drink, leading them toward the backyard or kitchen or wherever the action is, or literally popping an antipasto into their mouths upon their arrival. While these are all seemingly simple actions, a sensuous welcome makes us all feel more at home.

A quiet, stolen moment seen through a window: a nun sweeping up after a wedding—the bride and groom left the chapel in a swirl of rose petals.

Embrace Insieme *(Togetherness)*

—

Italians excel at togetherness, which they call *insieme*; no matter where you go throughout Italy, you'll find countless groups of old men drinking *cappuccini* in town squares, teenage girls walking with cones of gelato, or big families dining alfresco on pasta and wine. Perhaps what I love most about Italian gatherings is that they're nearly always intergenerational— grandfathers kiss babies while aunts chat with adolescent nephews, and grandmothers chop vegetables as their middle-aged sons select the wine. Gathering with all ages affirms that from the very young to the very old, everyone has an important place at the table. And because we're enthralled by different things at different ages, these get-togethers also help us notice things that might otherwise go untasted, unseen, unheard, unfelt, or unsmelled. Small children pay attention to birds in the trees, teens hum the latest pop songs, adults fixate on the taste of roasted lamb, and grandparents take pleasure in the sun's warmth and the scent of lavender in the air.

While the wabi-sabi concept often takes shape in quieter, more Zen-like practices (like sweeping the floor as a way of meditating, or drinking tea in the morning silence), I think it's also about celebrating life in these communal experiences where everyone is honored and appreciated— whether young or old, wise or innocent, single or married, with children or without. Wabi-sabi means living in tune with one another and being humbly aware that everyone has something to offer, no matter their age or experience. I've discovered that whenever I'm feeling overwhelmed by my own problems, I only have to spend time with small children or the elderly to revive my senses and be reminded that I'm just a tiny piece in a world much bigger than me.

Togetherness can be as uncomplicated as a potluck at the park or an open-door policy for friends on Friday evenings. Maybe it means a weekly dinner with extended family, or a monthly Sunday dinner if parents live farther away. If you don't have relatives living close by, try to establish a local family through a multi-generational group of friends. You might meet older or younger friends through work, or by volunteering, going to a place of worship, or walking around your neighborhood. Embracing family and intergenerational togetherness, like the Italians do so naturally, wakes us up to the wonders to be discovered at every age and stage of life.

The Sensuous Home

Fill Your Home with Fragrance

—

Smell is indelibly linked to memory; even subtle fragrances can bring us instantly back to a moment, a person, or a place, whether or not we were aware of a lingering aroma at the time. Italy is abundantly fragrant, and nearly every place I've been has left me with something sweet to remember it by. Whenever I catch a hint of orange blossom, I'm transported back to Sorrento, a city on the Mediterranean where the streets are lined with orange trees and their essence fills the air. A whiff of wisteria summons me to a flowering convent courtyard in Orvieto, and the warm, earthy scent of roasted chestnuts is firmly tied to Florence and the street vendors on every corner. I've always loved the feeling of walking into a familiar place or hugging a close friend and being overwhelmed by all the good associations that come with the smell, and I think this sensation can be powerfully comforting.

The same idea can be infused into your home with a fragrance that exemplifies *you* and how you want your space to feel. My Pacific Northwest friends have homes that smell of cedar, vetiver, leather, and wood smoke, and in California, my favorite homes emanate the aroma of freshly washed laundry, jasmine, and tuberose. Flooding your home with scent is the easy part—you can try candles, diffusers, room spray, real flowers, incense, or even just simmering water with a few drops of essential oil in it (which is one of my favorite ways to lightly infuse a space with fragrance). As with all things wabi-sabi, it's important to stick close to nature; instead of overly sweet, syrupy combinations that come entirely from a test tube, I usually gravitate toward naturally occurring, single-origin smells like lavender, eucalyptus, geranium, sandalwood, vanilla, coconut, rose, cinnamon, citrus, gardenia, or other similarly earthy scents. Everyone has a different sense of smell, however, so find something that works for you and make it your signature scent, or at least your seasonal go-to. Whether you're hosting an intimate or grand occasion, casual or fancy, mellow or lively, utilizing scent is a beautiful way to leave an impression and thoroughly amuse the senses.

OPPOSITE

*Stefano Gazzura prepares for the ensuing dinner by
sharpening his knives and slicing a variety of cured
meats for the table. The simple arrangements were made
of flowers and foliage collected from the garden and
whatever was growing along the road.*

*Infuse Special Occasions
with Festivity*

—

Italians truly know how to party, and by this I mean they celebrate special occasions with flair, be it a religious holiday or a nephew's birthday. They rely on symbolism, ritual, and a bit of whimsy to mark meaningful milestones in memorable ways. Some of my favorite recollections in Italy involve holy festival days, when processionals of traditionally dressed townsfolk pulled barrels of wine-for-all through the streets, or when everyone observed the day after Easter, called Pasquetta ("little Easter"), with large picnics in the countryside. I've also been a part of celebrations in honor of newly finished roof renovations, the arrival of spring, and visitors in town. These days are worth acknowledging not merely because they represent important anniversaries but because people also set aside time, energy, and enthusiasm to honor even more mundane occurrences in a remarkable way.

Thankfully, making an occasion extraordinary doesn't require months of planning, let alone hiring a rental company and a DJ; all it demands is a bit of thoughtfulness. A good rule of thumb is to consider all the senses and think about how you might appeal to each one. Different events and personalities call for varying forms of festivity, but some of my tried-and-true ways for inspiring celebration are hanging lights, having a fire (indoors or out), making a custom playlist, picking a seasonally appropriate scent (simmering spicy apple cider in winter or floral essential oils in spring), and filling the house with things like foraged arrangements or garlands, lots of candles, or an assortment of exceptional foods.

A willingness to stray from routine is perhaps the most important part of creating festivity. As much as I encourage you to delight in the mundane, extra-special occasions shared with friends and family are excellent opportunities to go all out. That said, "all out" is a relative term: it might simply mean cooking a well-loved but infrequently made meal and topping it off with a special beverage, an ice-cream sundae, and good old-fashioned dance music. Maybe the unexpected element is setting up a table in the backyard, arranging pillows and throws on the floor, or doing something unique for your guests, such as presenting each with a small gift, a poem, or a treat to take home. It's crucial to keep in mind (as wabi-sabi continually reminds us) that the aim is never perfection. Finding festivity doesn't mean resorting to what's expensive, lavish, or trendy; it just means creating something that is heartfelt, personal, and meaningful for you, and hopefully for your guests, too.

Set the Mood with Music

—

We all know that music—especially the right music—can radically alter our experiences; as with smell, we strongly associate it with particular feelings and memories we can't always express verbally. The sadness of a breakup becomes encapsulated in a Ryan Adams album; the freedom of a road trip is conveyed by a Bob Dylan compilation. Music creates a totally "sensational" experience that helps us be more present and aware of whatever is happening around us, no matter the setting or occasion.

While Italy obviously isn't the only place that delights in musical accompaniment, we only have to imagine an accordionist playing alongside a romantic pasta dinner to recognize that Italians excel at sensuous ambience. When I'm planning a get-together, whether it's a lunch with my parents or a dinner party for twelve, I often picture the whole scenario as if it's a film playing out before me. Setting the mood when we entertain is actually quite similar to setting a scene, since it's all about creating an environment that

evokes certain feelings, like coziness, calmness, or total exuberance. While we may not be able to accompany every life event with music, we *can* shape the mood of our shared occasions by picking a fitting sound track, whether we're going for the drama of instrumental or the coolness of jazz. With so much music available to us these days, there's no reason why we shouldn't be particular about how we "score" our gatherings.

If you're not sure where to start, think of a handful of adjectives that describe the way you want your occasion to feel or how you want to feel as you're hosting. Happy, lighthearted, playful, nostalgic, elegant, mysterious, romantic; each of these feelings conjures a different type of music. With just a bit of thoughtful exploration and selection, you can completely transform a nice occasion into a series of deeply felt, cinematic moments.

The Sensuous Table
Cook with Color
—

Cooking with color brings a palpable sense of celebration and beauty to the table, and while bright hues don't fall into the traditional wabi-sabi scheme, being mindful of colorful foods inspires seasonal eating, which in turn keeps us better in tune with what nature provides at the appropriate times—which *is* a very wabi-sabi way of being. Wabi-sabi encourages us to embrace how fleeting and transient everything is, including how short certain growing seasons are. As you may have noticed, each chapter has highlighted the importance of cooking locally and seasonally (and organically, when possible), and for good reason! Being conscientious consumers simplifies our options, not to mention makes us more aware of how, when, and where things grow. The tart taste of pale strawberries grown in November will never match the full pleasure of late-spring and early-summer varieties, a reminder that regardless of how antsy we get, seasonal foods are worth the wait. If something is at its most vibrant and flavorful, that's a good indication it's in peak season, so if we have a table or picnic blanket arrayed with a variety of hues, we're likely doing pretty well.

Even though many of Italy's staple foods come in rather muted tones—think of the beiges and blonds of pasta, bread, mozzarella, and white wine—the Italian table is full of color. Olive oil alone comes in a variety of shades, from pale yellows to brilliant greens, while vibrantly hued tomatoes, apricots, asparagus, plums, olives, eggplant, pistachios, melons, figs, lemons, and spinach create a dazzling spectrum. Cooking with color enriches the tasting palate as much as the visual palette: when, for example, you bite into a peach-colored melon wrapped in pink-tinged prosciutto and flecked with bright green mint or basil, these colors help signal to your mind that you're enjoying something thoroughly spectacular.

Let Flavors Speak for Themselves

—

Wabi-sabi always champions simplicity, and we can practice this in the kitchen by letting flavors sing on their own instead of masking them with unnecessarily complex combinations. My experience with Italian food is that it's nearly always a feast of essential flavors that don't require a lot of finagling, like the singular taste of ripe tomatoes, black truffles, Parmesan cheese, sage, arugula, balsamic vinegar, and hazelnuts. I recall a deceptively bland-looking but perfectly delicious pasta dish, seasoned with a bit of red pepper flakes; breakfasts of fig jam, spreadable cheese, and sweet crackers; square slices of *pizza bianca*, strong with thinly sliced onion; white bread slathered with fresh pesto made moments before. Keeping dishes and flavors uncomplicated is a nod to the wabi-sabi principle of doing more with less, teaching us to cook with economy while still celebrating flavors in their fullness.

I think we feel especially inclined to dress everything up when entertaining, but instead, use hosting as an opportunity to pare down. Make grapefruit wedges your appetizer, or perhaps a bowl of ripe grapes. Drizzle fresh tomato slices with just olive oil and a sprinkling of salt, and serve them as a side dish. Try keeping your entrée simple by limiting your pasta, meat, soup, or salad to just one or two dominant flavors. Buy a pint of gelato and eat it as is for dessert, or make *affogato* (vanilla gelato with a splash of espresso poured over the top). By drawing out exceptional flavors, we give our senses a chance to luxuriate in just one thing at a time. And these days, that's a welcome pleasure.

Linger at the Table

—

Idling around the table is a beautiful pastime shared by people all over the world, but with our increasingly busy, fragmented lives, it's difficult to be together without countless interruptions and distractions. Not long after I began planning dinners professionally, I discovered that many guests were more interested in taking photographs of their food or "sharing" their experience than they were in engaging with other people at the table. Likewise, it can be difficult to dine out these days without feeling rushed, as restaurants try to turn their tables as quickly as possible. Not so in Italy! Italians are expert lingerers, whether eating at home or at a trattoria, which becomes painfully obvious when you suddenly realize the surrounding locals are still working on their antipasto while you're anxiously summoning the waiter to bring the bill. Here, the focus is on the immersive experience of tasting, talking, and listening—rather than on quickly getting your fill of food or rushing to broadcast the event midstream. When we *linger*, it's because we are consciously savoring the moment, hoping the experience won't quickly come to an end.

Like so many other parts of life, we miss something important if we fail to truly "show up" at the table—and once we're there, to settle in and stay for a while. Breaking bread together gives us a chance to pause, look around at one another, and be grateful for what we have. It's an opportunity to set aside stresses and simply dwell in the present moment, which we can do much more easily if we're entirely captivated by our setting. As hosts, we can create this kind of enveloping experience with a thoughtful, sensory environment, but also by modeling how to slow down and simply be. Lingering means allowing dinners to roll late into the night or brunching long into the day, without rushing to clear the table or clean a haphazard kitchen. It means putting aside the laundry, errands, phone calls, text messages, or social media and instead letting ourselves be entirely swept up in togetherness.

Whether you're a host or a guest, some simple but useful tricks for relaxing at the table are to hide or turn off your gadget(s) entirely, take off your watch if you're a chronic time-checker, and quickly remind yourself of your priorities before you gather. Don't make other commitments surrounding your meal, since these will limit your ability to totally unwind. Give yourself a day or two afterward to deal with the cleanup and re-organization of the house. Being aware of what's ultimately important makes it easier to say no to possible distractions along the way and to focus on the people and place at hand. Moments like these, in which we "lose" ourselves, are often the most long-lasting, significant memories we have.

Take a Passeggiata

—

Immersing yourself in all the sights, sounds, and smells of your surrounding neighborhood and community can totally transform the way you feel about living there, creating the kind of attentive presence that wabi-sabi encourages. The loveliest tradition I've witnessed in Italy (and there are many) that inspires such immersion is the daily ritual of *passeggiata*—an all-ages evening stroll through the village or city streets; friends, young and old, walk together down cobblestone walkways, or simply sit on piazza benches as others mosey by. Italians consider passeggiata a time to congregate with friends or family, as well as to visit shopkeepers, decompress from the day, or purchase last-minute items for dinner. It's a form of taking table-gathering out onto the streets, but in a completely communal, everyone's-invited kind of way—and without the table. This regular occurrence is the ultimate expression of shared leisure, where instead of tuning out in front of the television (which can also be a necessary luxury), people gather to connect face-to-face, arm in arm. Instead of chat rooms, Instagram, or Tinder, there's gossip on street corners and flirting over cones of gelato. While the walk itself may be a lazy amble, Italians take passeggiata seriously, usually dressing up and treating it as a real occasion. It's something like the American tradition of the block party except that it happens every day, and everywhere.

While block parties seem to be few and far between these days (at least where I live), the closest thing I've experienced to passeggiata outside of Italy is at our weekly farmers' markets or on big holidays, when my family often takes a walk on the beach following an afternoon feast. It seems everyone has the same idea on these days, as we run into friends and families from both around the neighborhood and across town. It's an opportunity for catching up, slowing down, and simply enjoying the beauty of communal togetherness in real time, without the help (or hindrance) of technology. These special moments when the community gathers in the same place at the same time always leave me with a deep sense of belonging and a feeling of pride in this shared place we call home.

We can bring the spirit of passeggiata into our own neighborhoods, towns, and cities, even if we're a long way from Italy and its accepted traditions; all this requires is the desire to step outside and connect with others around you in person on a regular basis. Maybe this simply means going on walks in an effort to meet your neighbors, inviting friends who live nearby to join you for evening strolls, or planning frequent meet-ups in the park. Perhaps you go as far as initiating a casual potluck for everyone on your street, hosting your own version of a block party. Whatever the case, I've discovered that knowing my neighbors and being connected to the people I live among makes me feel safer, more at home, and more deeply rooted to my community at large. While the Internet has done wonders for connecting us, participating in the here and now is vital to experiencing real, sensuous beauty and joy in the spaces where we've settled. In true wabi-sabi fashion, adopting our own form of passeggiata helps us be more sensuously present wherever we live.

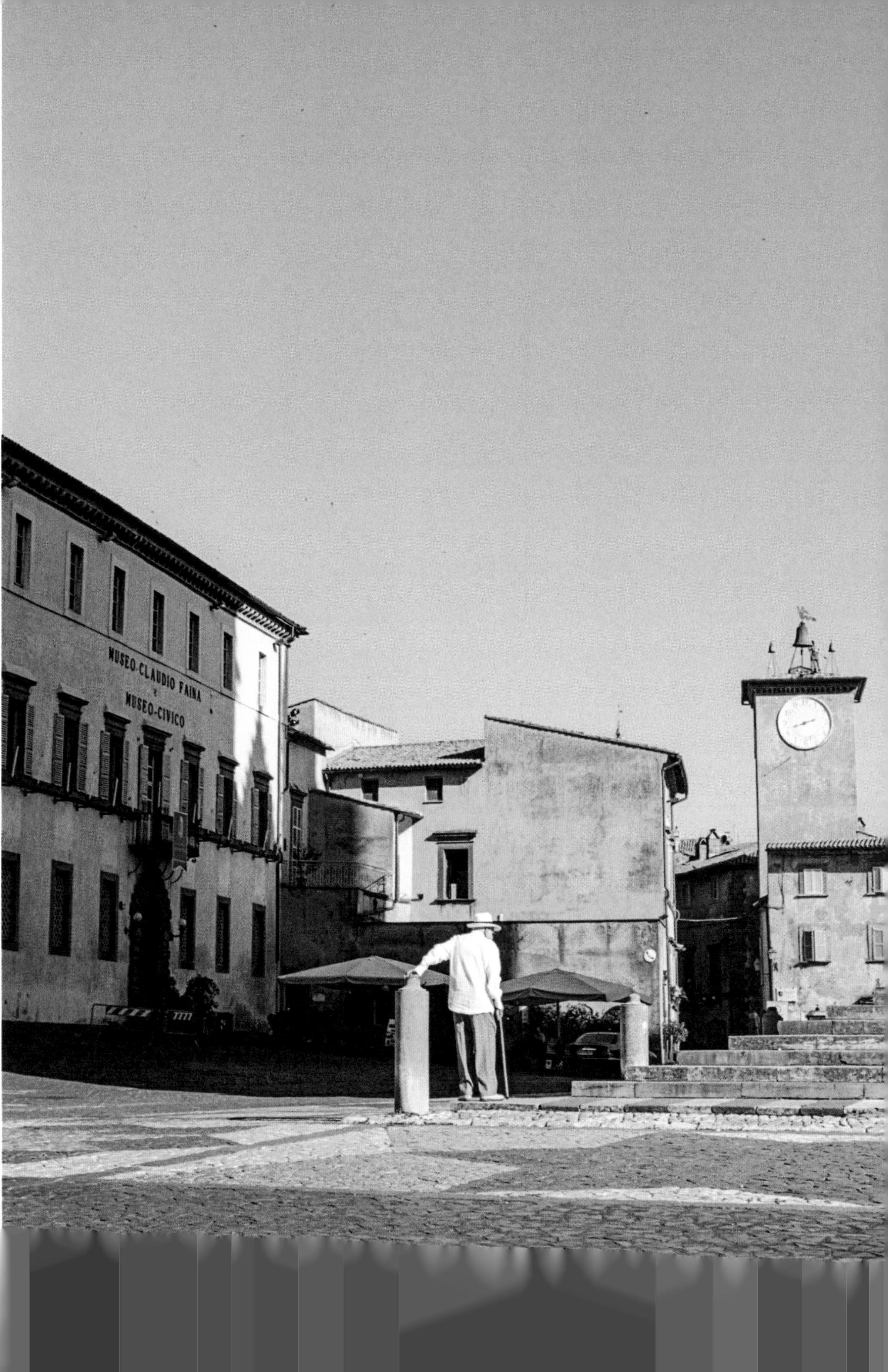
MUSEO CLAUDIO FAINA
E
MUSEO CIVICO

PRACTICAL MATTERS

Don't hold back when greeting your guests. Kiss them on the cheeks; give a warm hug or handshake; share an anecdote that made you think of them that week . . . whatever it is, do it with warm enthusiasm.

—

Find ways to incorporate friends of all ages into your gatherings. Invite families with young children over for dinner (especially if you don't have any yourself), or extend a brunch invitation to your grandmother if she lives close by.

—

Invest in a few scents that you love having around the house, whether that means buying a gardenia plant or picking up a candle or two. Start taking advantage of smell as a way to elevate your day, whether at home alone or while having dinner with a pal.

—

Next time you have a special occasion to celebrate, like a birthday, anniversary, or graduation, consider one or two ways you might make it especially festive. For example, ask each guest to come with a story to share about the birthday girl, prepare a nostalgic menu that has significance to you and your guests, or throw a May Day brunch and send your friends home with flowers.

—

Take a quiet night at home to craft a few playlists that might come in handy down the road. I always name my playlists based on specific seasons or moods, so when I have guests over I know what will be most fitting for the company and the occasion.

—

Dress up your table with colorful foods, making choices based on what's seasonally available. Keep in mind that the more (naturally occurring) colors you have on the table, the more vitamins and nutrients you're likely absorbing as well!

—

Stick to a menu that celebrates simple flavors. There's no need to pick the most complicated recipes; instead, select a few dominant flavors that work well together, and use those to shape your meal.

—

Some days require us to rush through eating, but when you have friends or family over for a meal, commit to mellowing out at the table. Have another plate of food, glass of wine, or piece of pie—whatever it takes to slow you down.

—

Start taking an evening walk around your neighborhood before or after dinner. Stop and chat with familiar faces, or pop by the houses of friends who live nearby and invite them along for a stroll. Participating fully in the place where you live (noticing unique trees, smelling flowers, taking new walking routes, meeting your neighbors) will invigorate you to experience everything around you in a new way.

SETTING THE TABLE

As with everything Italian-inspired, the table should be entirely sensuous, full of lovely but simple sights and smells. Bowls of lemons or apricots, a vase full of fragrant basil or lavender stalks, a dish or decanter of bright green olive oil—all of these will bring liveliness to the table without overdoing it. What makes an Italian meal memorable is rarely the decor, which is often quite understated, but rather the exquisite combination of flavors and colors that appeal to all of the senses. Instead of putting your energy into a grand tablescape, channel your efforts into a bright and flavorful homemade pesto, pizza, or tomato sauce. If you're feeling especially adventurous (and have plenty of time on your hands), try making your own pasta. You won't be disappointed by the smell and taste of the results, even if it looks a bit wonky. Accompany one bigger cooking effort (like pizza, pasta, or a meat dish) with some easier dishes and starters that can be assembled in a jiffy.

Melon and Prosciutto with Mint or Basil and White Balsamic Vinegar

It's best to use an orange-fleshed melon for this combo, so look for cantaloupe, orange-fleshed honeydew, sugar kiss, Crenshaw, and so on.

Cut the melon in half and scoop out the seeds. Slice into wedges, or smaller pieces if you prefer, and cut these in half lengthwise. I usually trim the peel from the wedges at this point, but you can also remove the peel at the beginning of the process.

Toss the wedges or half-wedges in a bowl with 2 to 3 tablespoons of white balsamic vinegar (a not-so-sweet melon will require less vinegar), a dash of salt, and very thin strips of fresh mint or basil leaves. Once the melon wedges are coated in this thin syrup, wrap each wedge in a piece of prosciutto roughly 1 to 2 inches wide (you can slice or simply rip the pieces down to size).

Plate and serve!

OPPOSITE

For this particular version, I used both pumpkin butter and a bit of fig jam for the base. I also included slices of fennel sausage and prosciutto. It was delicious!

Fig or Pumpkin Pizza

I first fell in love with figs (and fig jam) while in Italy, and also experienced my first pumpkin-based pizza at a little pizzeria in Orvieto called Charlie's. Both have been favorites ever since. This recipe is always a winner even with the most traditional pizza-lovers.

Whether you're going the fig or pumpkin route, start by finding a pizza dough recipe or a premade dough, and preheat the oven according to the recipe or package instructions, usually to between 400 and 500°F. Stretch and shape your dough on a baking sheet, or if you have a pizza stone, make sure you have a way to easily slide the assembled dough onto the warmed stone (like a paddle or well-floured parchment paper). If the dough is a bit thick even after being stretched, I suggest prebaking it for 7 to 10 minutes before adding any toppings.

If you're making a fig pizza, use a fig jam as the base or fresh figs as a topping. If you're using a fig jam base, first slather a bit of olive oil (1 to 2 tablespoons) onto the dough with the back of a spoon, then sprinkle with flaky salt. Next, spoon a thin layer of fig jam evenly over the surface.

If you opt to use fresh figs as the topping, add a touch of flavor to the olive oil by first whisking it together with maple syrup or honey, a pinch of salt, and crushed garlic (a clove or two will do).

If you're using a pumpkin base, use the same process as with the fig jam. I suggest using a pumpkin butter since this will already be seasoned and tasty, versus just straight pumpkin puree, which is far less appealing (I speak here from experience).

For the topping of either pizza, layer a soft cheese like crumbly goat, ricotta, burrata, or fresh buffalo mozzarella onto the base. It's not necessary to completely cover the base like you would with grated mozzarella—just generously dot the surface with crumbles, clumps, or slices.

Adding a protein is optional, of course, but I like slices of soppressata salami, prosciutto, or fennel sausage, sliced or crumbled and browned, on my pizza. I also like adding thinly sliced red onion or shallots at this stage.

Finally, top the pizza with a heaping pile of spinach or arugula. This is also when you scatter sliced fresh figs (halved or quartered) over the surface if you're making a fig pizza. Feel free to drizzle more olive oil over everything, or use the olive oil and syrup mixture, if the pizza looks a little dry.

Baking time depends on whether you prebaked or not. If you did, the pizza will need only 5 to 10 minutes in a hot oven. Check frequently to make sure you don't overcrisp.

Affogato

There's hardly a simpler dessert to prepare than affogato. It's the Italian word for "drowned," and it consists of just a scoop or two of gelato doused with a shot of espresso. It's getting easier and easier to find good gelato in the States, but ice cream can work, too.

My preference is to use plain vanilla, chocolate, or coffee gelato, but experiment as you like. Make sure to scoop it into a glass or mug that can handle hot liquid, and then pour espresso or coffee (about 3 tablespoons) over the top. If you feel like frilling it up just a touch, top with shaved chocolate, nuts, or dried coconut.

EPILOGUE

If you have made it this far, it should be obvious that this book is about coming together, no matter the time or place. My hope is that these pages inspire you to let down your guard and stop hiding behind the need to make things (and yourself) *perfect* before you throw open the doors on entertaining. Learning to celebrate, and then imitate, the wabi-sabi beauty that exists all around us uncomplicates our efforts and eliminates our fear of failure. If you leave behind these barriers and begin regularly sharing yourself and your home, you will discover that people step into your life in a surprising, reanimating way.

In my own experience—whether at home, at rest, or at work as an art director and writer—a wabi-sabi spirit has allowed me to ignore all the "shoulds" and instead move toward whatever brings me childlike joy. Among other things, this means I regularly serve meals on the floor, make bouquets of dried weeds, leave my doors open and windows screenless, and fill my home with simple belongings that ground me. Everyone will have their own version of what wabi-sabi liberates them to do or be, but the message is the same: Draw the very most out of very little and make something magical out of the mundane. Strip away the unnecessary and live in a mindful, uncluttered way. By uncluttered I mean physically uncluttered, but more important, mentally uncluttered—letting the main thing be the main thing. For me, the main thing is experiencing extraordinary moments of connection with others, and making a humble sanctuary in which to do so.

We are all hosts. We instinctively know how to "hang out," listen, sit in silence, pay attention, feed each other, eat together, and so on, because we are communal creatures. So go and do it. Become the welcoming face and create the warm home you long for—in the service of others—and do so with the carefree ease of one who knows it need not be perfect.

RESOURCES

Food Blogs, Cookbooks, and Magazines

101 Cookbooks

101cookbooks.com
Super Natural Cooking
Super Natural Every Day
Near & Far

I reference Heidi Swanson's vegetarian blog most often for wholesome breakfast ideas and desserts, but she has recipes for any time of day and all kinds of meals. I appreciate Swanson's approach because she cooks healthfully using whole ingredients, without getting caught up in worrying about too much fat, too many carbs, and so on. Instead, she takes a holistic approach to eating, drawing on foods found all over the world to create wholesome, filling meals for the entire family.

My New Roots

mynewroots.org
My New Roots: Inspired Plant-Based Recipes for Every Season

Sarah Britton's site has produced some of my very favorite go-to recipes for healthier (vegetarian, gluten-free, and often vegan) versions of longtime favorites—like rich fudgy brownies made entirely of dates and nuts—and simply good go-to meals for any day, like her Four Corners Lentil Soup (one of my fall and winter staples). While some of her recipes and ingredients (e.g., mung bean fettuccine) may be a bit intimidating, if you're less concerned with things like gluten, you can easily substitute ingredients to your liking. I find her site to be great when I want to step outside my comfort zone just a bit.

Sprouted Kitchen

sproutedkitchen.com
The Sprouted Kitchen: A Tastier Take on Whole Foods
The Sprouted Kitchen: Bowl + Spoon

Sara Forte's vegetarian blog and cookbooks are similarly focused on cooking wholesome, healthful meals for both adults and little ones (she has two kids of her own). I often refer to her site for salad recipes or to get out of whatever cooking rut I happen to be in. Sara posts only vegetarian recipes, but I regularly add my desired protein to her dishes to bulk them up. Her pancake recipe in *The Kinfolk Table* is an all-time favorite for Saturday mornings at home.

Donna Hay

donnahay.com.au

The New Easy (and many, many others!)

The first cookbook I regularly started cooking from was one by Donna Hay. She has wonderfully simple recipes for even the most novice cook or baker that are delicious, healthful, and perfect for feeding a crowd.

Food 52

food52.com

Food52 is a "food community" with a huge variety of recipes by many contributing chefs. I like this resource because the site has filtering options to find exactly what type of recipe you want, even if you don't know precisely what you're looking for; for example, you can filter your main ingredient to be anything from pork, to fruit, to chocolate.

Bon Appétit

bonappetit.com

Bon Appétit is one of those tried-and-true sources you know you can always count on for a quick fix, whether cooking for two or thirty. I love that they have online stories like "32 Easy Pastas for Weeknight Dinners" because, honestly, sometimes an easy pasta is all I can muster on a Tuesday evening.

Go-Tos for Home Basics

Muji

muji.com/us

I rely on Muji for simple, unassuming office supplies like pens, stationery, and notebooks, as well as for great organizational items like folders and boxes. This Japanese company's name actually means "without brand," or is short for "brandless quality goods"—which is exactly what you'll find there.

IKEA

ikea.com/us/en

I love IKEA for helping get my life in order with items like baskets, nice-looking utilitarian pieces (like brooms, step stools, toilet-paper-roll holders, bathroom organizers, and patio furniture), and practical goods for the kitchen. For instance, I stock up on sturdy IKEA glasses for when we have larger events or parties at home.

H&M Home

hm.com/us/department/HOME

I only recently discovered that H&M Home has beautiful linen bedding for great prices. Getting a few pieces here has allowed me to have a couple of different sheet sets and an extra duvet cover to switch out when my fancier (i.e., more expensive) bedding is in the wash.

Go-Tos for Superspecial Home Items (i.e., Things You're Willing to Save Up For or Splurge On)

Spartan

Austin, TX; San Francisco, CA; and Portland, OR

spartan-shop.com

Spartan is one of my favorite places for buying gifts or finding extra-special items for my own home, like candles, mugs, or one-of-a-kind vases. Spartan currently has three physical locations, but most of what owner/buyer Currie Person carries can also be found in the online shop.

Alder & Co.

Portland, OR, and Germantown, NY

alderandcoshop.com

Alder & Co. is, by their own terms, an "upscale boutique" that takes cues from both French and Japanese style/design. While it's probably not for everyday shopping (at least not for most of us), owners Carla Helmholz and Rebecca Westby have curated a beautiful space (both physical and online) for unique, timeless treasures like luxurious blankets, waffle-weave towels, and home accent pieces.

Brook Farm General Store

East Hampton, NY

brookfarmgeneralstore.com

This general store is the epitome of combining functionality and beauty. Carrying everything from gardening tools to linen carryalls to wall hooks, this could be a one-stop shop for outfitting your home with hardworking, lovely things, just as the name implies. I especially love their in-house line of ceramics, called Tourne.

Kaufmann Mercantile

Brooklyn, NY

kaufmann-mercantile.com

Similar to Brook Farm, Kaufmann Mercantile stocks a wide range of items for the home and the body. A great resource for dressing up your tabletop, bathroom, or desk with well-made, superlative items.

Joinery

Brooklyn, NY

joinerynyc.com

I love Joinery primarily for its blankets, woven rugs, and floor mats. They do carry lovely practical home goods as well, like mugs, scrub brushes, and kitchen utensils. Perfect for finding beautifully useful items.

Caroline Z Hurley

Brooklyn, NY

carolinezhurley.com

Caroline Hurley designs fun and playful block-printed linens (napkins, tablecloths, throws, pillowcases, etc.) that bring a bit of color and lightness into your home. She also designs exquisitely simple but unique hand-sewn quilts that I've been eyeing for years.

Parachute Home

Venice, CA

parachutehome.com

A perfect source for high-quality bedding and towels that are made to last. After sleeping on exclusively IKEA sheets (which were perfectly comfortable and utilitarian) during my twenties, upgrading to this linen bedding set felt like a real luxury.

Block Shop Textiles

blockshoptextiles.com

Owned and run by two sisters, Block Shop works with a group of master weavers in Bagru, India, to create beautiful hand-block-printed textiles and rugs. Any of their items adds a gorgeous handmade touch to the floor, couch, or wall.

Inspiring Interior Designers

Ilse Crawford

studioilse.com

Ilse Crawford is a brilliant designer whose work is always about creating spaces that function for life, and prioritizing the human experience rather than solely worrying about how things look. Her book *A Frame for Life* is a beautiful collection of past projects that her design studio, Studioilse, has worked on over the years, whether personal homes or retail spaces, restaurants or hotels. Crawford's collaboration with IKEA also produced some of my favorite IKEA pieces ever!

John Pawson

johnpawson.com

John Pawson falls into the category of extreme minimalism, but his simplicity and creative use of light is always a surprise. If you're prone to decorating with *too much*, looking at his work can be an inspirational antidote.

Studio KO

studioko.fr

While technically an architectural firm studio, this pair of French designers who are partners in work and life create beautifully thoughtful spaces, inside and out. Although their projects include much more sleek and lavish homes than I am sure to ever live in, I enjoy referencing their work as examples of pared-back but comfortable spaces to aspire to.

Further Reading on Wabi-Sabi

Wabi-Sabi for Artists, Designers, Poets & Philosophers by Leonard Koren

This book has been my constant go-to inspiration for learning about wabi-sabi, understanding where it comes from, and discovering how to embody its principles in my own life. Koren's writings have served as my wabi-sabi guidebook for many years, and his books were by my side the whole time I worked on this collection.

Wabi-Sabi: Further Thoughts by Leonard Koren

This is Koren's 2015 follow-up to his first book on wabi-sabi, which was written in 1994. This volume goes a bit more in depth into the history of wabi-sabi and how it came to be.

Wabi Sabi: The Japanese Art of Impermanence by Andrew Juniper

I found this book to be a helpful sidekick to Leonard Koren's books, by fleshing out the concept in a handful of ways.

Wabi Sabi by Mark Reibstein

This delightful children's book about a cat named Wabi Sabi is as enlightening for adults as it is for children. With beautiful accompanying collages, the simple text and haiku woven throughout uncover the wabi-sabi worldview.

THANK-YOUS

Thanks, first and foremost, to my family for supporting me in countless ways throughout this adventure. To Ryan, for being the best "assistant" one could ask for. To Mom and Dad for being early proofreaders and sounding boards, and for providing a quiet house in which to write and daydream this book into being. To Katie, Kristy, Alex, and Elodie for being tireless encouragers and cheerleaders from near and far.

A debt of gratitude to my editor, Shoshana Gutmajer, and publisher, Lia Ronnen, for believing in me, always pushing me to do better, and helping to make this project one that I am proud to share. Thanks to the entire Artisan team—especially Mura Dominko, Michelle Ishay-Cohen, Jane Treuhaft, Sibylle Kazeroid, Nancy Murray, Allison McGeehon, and Theresa Collier—for enabling this book to come to fruition with all its parts and pieces.

Big thanks to Susie Finesman, for your continued wisdom and constant encouragement along the way.

To Rebecca Flint Marx—thank you for your endless patience and deft ability to refine my words, finesse my sentences, and help me write as simply as possible. I am deeply grateful for your support throughout the writing process.

Thanks to Charlotte Heal, for your brilliant design work and endlessly creative solutions at every turn.

Thank you to the handful of talented friends who told me I could do this—especially those who encouraged me to photograph this project myself. You know who you are.

This book wouldn't have been possible without the generosity of the people who opened their homes and lives to Ryan and me, offering hospitality in a multitude of forms. Thank you for letting us photograph your homes, your faces, your families, and the beautiful way you live your lives. To everyone who participated in this book in some fashion—whether at the table, behind the scenes, or otherwise—thank you for playing a crucial role, however big or small. I honestly couldn't have done it without you.

In Japan: Giant thanks to Tina Minami Dhingra, who helped orchestrate a whirlwind tour of Japan, introducing us to beautiful places and people everywhere we went. Thank you to Chieko Ueno; Kimiko Hiyamizu; Kyoko Ide and the whole team at YAECA; Reiko Ohhashi; Yuko Watanabe; Nobuyuki and Erina Kosuge; Masayo Funakoshi; Akiko Shingu; Yuri Nomura; Yukari Iki; Hiroko Nomura; and Nanao Kobayashi.

In Denmark: Very special thanks to Mikkel, Camilla, Oscar, Alma, Konrad, and Viggo Karstad for sharing both your incredible kindness and your extended family with us. Thank you to Cecilie Milsted Lind and Troels Nyboe Andersen; Vibeke Rudolph and Bjarne Karstad; Tinna Milsted and Manuel Sanchez; and Jessica Gray and Luc Fuller.

In California: My gratitude goes to Joya Rose and Jesse Groves; Hannah Pearl Utt; Cara Bonewitz; Meg Callahan; Jordan Thomas; Mikaila Allison; Wanda Weller; Arley Sakai; Seal Graeber; Michele Rozo; Nanette Stowell; Kourtney Morgan; Rene Norman; Jeanne Heckman; Karis Van Noord (and Hanz); Annemarie and Lukas Niklasson; Raleigh Clemens; Danielle and Ben Darin; Carissa, Andrew, Rinah, and River Gallo; and Jen, John, and Julien Vitale.

In France: Huge thanks to Chantal, Harry, and Sophie Dolman; Annie, Colin, Nikolas, and Lily Moore; Irene Espade; Sylvain Ferrai; and Andrew Trotter.

In Italy: Special thanks to John Skillen for being a gracious and generous coordinator in Orvieto and to Federico and Hannah Armbrust Badia; Gianna Scavo; Isabelle Skillen; Raffaela Franco and Stefano Gazzura; Thomas Jones; Giacomo and Anna Lardani; Alessandro, Emanuela Luciani, Michele, Daniele, Gabriele, and Gemma Lardani; and Kay and Csaba Borzsonyi.

INDEX

Page numbers in *italics* refer to picture captions.

acceptance of the inevitable, 126, 135
ages, gathering with people of all, 222, 249
air, 193, 203
artful living, 183

Badia, Federico and Hannah, *219*
beauty, 47, 203, 216
    unexpected, 27, 96, 101
    utility and, 95, 101
bowing, 34, 37, 61

California, 111–62
calm, from nature, 129, 153
Camellas-Lloret, *178*
candid, being, 118, 153
catastrophizing, 58
c'est la vie attitude, 176, *176*, 203
Child, Julia, 198, 204
child caves, 138, 153
Churchill, Winston, 136
clutter, 85, 101
coffee breaks, 78, 101
collecting and curating, 86, 101
colors:
    of food, 96, 101, 236, 249
    of nature, 129, 132–33, 153
community and neighborhood, 244, 249
coziness and homeyness, 89, 101, 114, 120

Denmark, 73–107
details, 126, 153
disasters, 58, 61, 120
Dussouchaud, Chantal, *176*

evening, 146, 153
    walks during, 244, 249

flowers, 47, *47*, 61
focusing on your guests, 27–28, 34
food and recipes, 57, 61, 101, 249
    æbleflæsk, 106
    affogato, 256
    all-season tacos, 159–60
    baked apples, 107

colors of, 96, 101, 236, 249
eating with your hands, 145
fancy toast, 206
fig or pumpkin pizza, 254–55
flavors of, 238, 249
French approach to, 204
ingredients, 196, 198, 203
melon and prosciutto with mint or basil
    and white balsamic vinegar, 253
mint and lemon salad, 161–62
one-bowl meals, 63
o-nigiri (rice balls), 69
oven-roasted chicken with green garlic, shallots,
    lemon, and thyme, 209
picnics, 150, 153, 154
roasted yams or sweet potatoes with butter and
    herbs, 208
sandwiches, 99, 101
seasonal, 236, 249
simple traditional noodles, 66
smørrebrød, 99, 104
stone fruit with honey-vanilla goat cheese, 156
tastes of, 198, 203
textures of, 101, 198, 203
wholesome bowl, 64
forts and hidden places, 138, 153
fragrance, 228, 249
France, 169–209
furniture, 194, 203

Gallo, Andrew, Carissa, Rinah, and River, *114*
Gazzura, Stefano, *232*
Granny, *198*
gratitude, 34, 37, 57, 136, 203, 241
greeting your guests, 219, 249
Groves, Joya Rose, *118*

habitual hosting, 80, 101
handmade items, 55, 61
hidden places, 138, 153
home, 24
homeyness and coziness, 89, 101, 114, 120
humble materials, 44, 61
humility, 34, 37, 50, 58
hygge, 76, 89

intimate spaces, 114
Italy, 213–56

Japan, 31–69
joy, 183, 203

Karstad, Mikkel and Camilla, 83
kindness, 118
kitchen, 120, 153
Koren, Leonard, 86

light, 193
linens, 186, 203

making do with what you have, 27
Mastering the Art of French Cooking (Child,
    Bertholle, and Beck), 198
material choices, 44, 61
morning, 146, 153
Moore, Annie, *178, 198*
Moore, Colin, *178*
music, 235
    playlists, 232, 235, 249

natural approach, 178, 203
nature, 172, 193
    calm and, 129, 153
    color and, 129, 132–33, 153
    decorating with, 190, 203
    see also outdoors
Nielsen, Holger, 95
Nobu and Erina, 37, *48*
Nomura, Yuri, *48*, 66

open-door policy, 135, 153
outdoors, 140, 193, 203
    picnics, 150, 153, 154
    see also nature

participation of guests, 28, 38
passeggiata, 244
Pattern Language, A (Alexander, Ishikawa,
    and Silverstein), 138
personal items, 136, 153
picnics, 150, 153 154
plants, 190, 203

practical matters, 61, 101, 153, 203, 249
preparation, 38, 61

questions, asking, 118, 153

Rapp, John, *129*

Sakai, Arley, *120, 153*
scents, 228, 249
senses, 216, 232, 238
shoes and slippers, 50, 61
simplicity, 76
slowing down, 41, 61
    lingering at the table, 241, 249
special occasions, 232, 249
stepping away from tasks, 78, 101

table:
    alternatives to eating at, 140, 153
    imperfections and stories attached to, 194
    lingering at, 241, 249
    setting, 63, 96, 101, 102, 154, 204, 250
time-outs, 153
time with others, 25
togetherness, 222
touch, 125, 153, 219

Ueno, Chieko, 47
unexpected:
    beauty, 27, 96, 101
    natural objects for practical needs, 190, 203
utility, 129
    beauty and, 95, 101

wabi-sabi:
    examples of what is and isn't, 20
    meaning of, 11, 18
*Wabi-Sabi for Artists, Designers, Poets &
    Philosophers* (Koren), 86
Weil, Simone, 34
Weller, Wanda, *120, 129, 153*

Zen gardens, 41

JULIE POINTER ADAMS has been casually entertaining friends for the better part of her life, but she began doing so professionally when she developed and directed *Kinfolk* magazine's original dinner and workshop series alongside editor Nathan Williams for several years. Julie has planned, hosted, and overseen hundreds of both small and not-so-small gatherings all over the world. She currently lives in Santa Barbara, California, with her husband, Ryan.

—

For more on *Wabi-Sabi Welcome*, visit wabisabiwelcome.com.